# The How and Why of Cookery

An O-level Cookery Course

# The How and Why of Cookery

By N. M. Haselgrove B.Sc. and K. A. Scallon B.Sc.

Extensively revised for the fourth edition
by Jennifer Kelly B.Sc.

Collins Educational

Fourth revised edition
First published 1981 by Hart-Davis Educational Ltd
Reprinted 1981, 1982 (twice), 1983
Published and reprinted 1984 by Collins Educational
Reprinted 1985, 1987

ISBN 0 00 327317 2

Published by Collins Educational
8 Grafton Street, London W1X 3LA



Book design by Ken Vail



Phototypeset by Filmtype Services Limited, Scarborough

Printed and bound in Great Britain by
Bell and Bain Ltd., Glasgow

# Contents

**The How and Why of Cookery**

This book is intended for use by candidates at ordinary level in the General Certificate of Education. It will help them to enjoy the theory of the work by making them curious about:

1. The *HOW* of the subject; that is, how the body deals with nutrients, general rules for preparation of food and methods of cooking, planning of meals and of kitchens.

2. The *WHY*; that is, practical reasons for these rules and scientific reasons for the methods given.

The book will give an interesting and instructive background to the study of food and nutrition at any level and, also, will be useful to those pupils not sitting for examinations.

It is not a recipe book.

# 1 Food and nutrition

*What food is  What nutrients are  How the body deals with nutrients  How nutrients in food behave  Energy*

The reason *why* we eat food is to keep alive and healthy. To find out *how* food does this, we need to understand what food is and how it behaves. Food is any substance which, when eaten, is absorbed by the body and used for growth and repair of tissues, production of energy or control of these processes.

## Nutrients

Nutrients are substances found in food which have a particular, specific function in the body. Thus some nutrients are used for growth and repair while others control the chemical changes in the body. To understand the functions of food we need to know the functions of each nutrient. There are six types:

| | |
|---|---|
| Proteins | Vitamins |
| Fats | Minerals |
| Carbohydrates | Water |

Foods usually consist of a mixture of these nutrients, e.g. milk contains some of each of these types of nutrients. Sugar contains only one, i.e. carbohydrate.

Chief uses of nutrients

1. *Growth and repair of tissues*: this needs proteins, minerals (especially iron and calcium) and vitamins C and D.
2. *Production of energy*: this needs carbohydrates, fats, or proteins with B vitamins.
3. *Control of body processes*: this needs minerals, all the vitamins, water and fibre.

## Proteins

There are many hundreds of different proteins that occur in food and in our bodies. Proteins are essential constituents of all cells, where they regulate the process of living or provide structure. The body proteins have to be made from those found in our food; the food proteins being taken in, broken down and rebuilt into body proteins. To understand this process we must know more about the nature of proteins.

Nature of proteins

Proteins are complex compounds made of the elements carbon, hydrogen, oxygen, nitrogen and, sometimes, sulphur and phosphorus. These chemical elements are grouped together into units called amino acids and a chain of amino acids forms a protein. In all, there are about twenty-two amino acids in the food we eat which, in varying numbers and combinations, form each of the hundreds of different proteins.

**Essential amino acids**

The body can change some of these amino acids in food to form others necessary for protein building. However, the remaining amino acids cannot be formed in this way and must come ready-made in the food we eat. These are called essential amino acids as it is essential that we obtain them from the proteins in our food.

To use an analogy, we can liken proteins to necklaces made up of coloured beads. The amino acids are the beads and those acids which can be made by the body from others in food are like green beads which could be made from blue and yellow ones. Other amino acids are like beads in the primary colours yellow and red, they cannot be synthesised and must come ready-made in our food.

**Complete and incomplete proteins**

If a protein contains all the essential amino acids in the right proportions for building our body proteins then it is said to be complete. It has a similar amino acid composition to that of our body proteins. These proteins are of high biological value and are usually of animal origin, e.g. the proteins in milk are complete.

If a protein lacks one or more of the essential amino acids then it is said to be incomplete. These proteins are of low biological value and are generally of plant origin, e.g. wheat proteins are low in the essential amino acid lysine.

**Pairing of proteins**

If we eat a mixture of proteins, then one may make up the shortage of an essential amino acid in the other, e.g. cereal and milk together provide enough of all the essential amino acids we need because milk supplies plenty of lysine. This is called the pairing or complementation of proteins. Similarly, if two proteins of low biological value are eaten together, the total value of the proteins is high, as the mixture supplies all the essential amino acids. Other examples of the pairing of proteins in food are beans on toast, bread and cheese, spaghetti bolognese, rice and peas.

**Sources of proteins**

Proteins are found in varying amounts in both animal and plant foods. In the average UK diet, one-third comes from plant sources and two-thirds from animal sources.

Animal foods such as meat, fish, eggs, milk and cheese supply most of the complete protein in our diet. They are the foods we usually choose to make the basis of a meal. The seeds of plants are storehouses containing useful amounts of incomplete protein and cereals and pulses are the main sources of this. Cereals include wheat, rice and maize. As wheat is a particularly good source of incomplete protein, wheat products such as bread, flour, breakfast cereals and pastry are specially important. Pulses are the mature seeds of the pea and bean family of plants. Many varieties of these are grown all over the world. They include soya beans, peas, lentils, dahls, kidney beans, haricot (baked) beans and groundnuts. Pulses supply lysine and so complement the protein in cereals such as rice and maize.

Proteins are chemical substances and any one food may contain several different proteins, e.g. milk contains caseinogen, lactoglobulin and lactalbumin. The following are examples of named proteins: myosin in meat, albumin in egg, casein in cheese, gliadin and glutenin in wheat, legumin in pulses. The above named foods do not contain proteins alone, they may also contain fats, carbohydrates, minerals, vitamins and water.

### Functions of proteins

Proteins are essential to life, every cell contains proteins; enzymes and hormones are proteins. We must eat proteins because the body can only make its own proteins from those contained in the diet. Proteins are used for:

1. *Growth*: especially in children and pregnant women. The food proteins are digested and the amino acids are absorbed into the bloodstream. The cells of the body then take the amino acids they need to make their own pattern of protein. So the food we eat must supply the right proportions of all the amino acids used for building our body proteins.
2. *Renewal*: all the cell proteins and secretions of enzymes and hormones need to be constantly renewed with fresh amino acids. People of all ages need proteins for renewal and secretions.
3. *Repair*: after illness, accidents or surgery, extra protein is needed for good and rapid recovery.
4. *Energy*: when the body has used all the amino acids it needs for construction, the remainder are deaminated in the liver, i.e. the nitrogen part of the molecule becomes urea and the rest of the molecule is 'burnt' or oxidised to produce energy (17 kJ/g). About 10–15% of our energy needs should be supplied by protein. Sufficient carbohydrate or fat should be eaten to provide the rest of our energy needs so that protein can be used for its most important functions of growth and renewal.

### Recommended protein intake

It is difficult to measure how much protein we need but a food supply in which 10% of the energy is provided by protein should be the target. In the UK the recommended daily intake (RDI) is as follows:

| | |
|---|---|
| Child of 1 year | 30 g |
| Child 7–8 years | 48 g |
| Girls 15–17 years | 53 g |
| Boys 15–17 years | 72 g |
| Women (most occupations) | 54 g |
| Men (moderately active) | 70 g |

A regular daily intake of protein is necessary as no spare amino acids can be stored in the body for use at a later time.

### Protein deficiency

If we do not eat enough protein, cells lack amino acids for growth and renewal. In children growth slows down or stops. There are digestive upsets as enzymes are not produced. The liver fails to function normally. The muscles become weak and so limbs are thin and the tummy is soft and may look distended.

As foods are mixtures of nutrients, we rarely find protein alone is missing. The result of a low intake of protein and other nutrients supplying energy is Protein-Energy Malnutrition (PEM). Kwashiorkor is a PEM disease occurring when a child is weaned from breast milk to a diet low in protein.

Behaviour of food proteins

Proteins can be denatured, that is the molecules lose their natural shape and become less soluble. This can be seen in sour milk where the caseinogen comes out of solution and forms curds. Egg white denatures and coagulates when heated above 60°C. Meat fibres shrink on heating and myoglobin, the red colour in meat, changes to brown.

Collagen, a protein in the connective tissue of meat, changes to soluble gelatin on heating in the presence of water, thus meat becomes tender when stewed.

Proteins can bind with water, as gelatin does in setting a jelly. Egg proteins thicken milk when the two are heated together, forming a custard. Water added to wheat proteins makes a sticky, elastic substance called gluten.

Some proteins can be whisked and will hold many bubbles of air in a foam, e.g. egg white.

Egg proteins can be used to stabilise an emulsion of vinegar and oil, e.g. mayonnaise.

The physical properties of proteins, stated above, are used during food preparation and cooking.

One chemical change that occurs in the cooking of some foods is the Maillard browning reaction. Proteins react with reducing sugars to produce a complex brown substance which has a pleasant flavour, aroma and colour and is seen in the crust of bread, in toast, breakfast cereals and meat extracts.
(See page 22 for details of the digestion and absorption of proteins.)

## Carbohydrates

Nature of carbohydrates

Carbohydrates are nutrients composed of three elements: carbon, hydrogen and oxygen, the latter two being in the same proportions as in water, hence 'hydrate'. There are three main groups of carbohydrates in food:

- Sugars
- Starches
- Unavailable carbohydrates or fibre

The sugars and starches can be used for energy. The unavailable carbohydrates consist of cellulose and related materials, they cannot be digested and used for energy.

Carbohydrates in the diet

1. *Sugars*: monosaccharides, e.g. glucose, fructose
   disaccharides, e.g. sucrose, lactose, maltose
2. *Starches*: polysaccharides, e.g. starches in cereals and potatoes
3. *Unavailable carbohydrates*: polysaccharides, e.g. cellulose in bran, pectin in fruit

1. *Sugars*

Simple sugars or monosaccharides consist of single sugar units. Glucose, or dextrose, is found in fruit and also in the blood of living animals (the result of the digestion of carbohydrates). It is less sweet than the disaccharide sucrose and is used in invalid drinks to increase the energy value. Fructose is a very sweet sugar found in small amounts in honey and fruit.

Disaccharides consist of two monosaccharides joined together. Glucose and fructose joined together make sucrose. This is the common sugar obtained from cane or beet. Glucose and galactose join together to form lactose (milk sugar). Two units of glucose form maltose (malt sugar).

2. *Starches*

Starches are polysaccharides, i.e. made of many units of glucose joined together. Starch forms grains of a size and shape that are characteristic for each type of plant. Starch from maize differs from wheat starch or potato starch. Starch is only found in plant foods, never in animal foods.

Glycogen is similar to starch, it is a polysaccharide that occurs in living animals. Small amounts are stored in the liver and muscles as an energy reserve. It is changed to glucose after an animal's death.

3. *Unavailable carbohydrates*

These substances, e.g. cellulose and pectin, are all polysaccharides and the sugar units are joined in such a way that our digestive enzymes are not able to break them down. They are also known as dietary fibre or roughage. (See page 16.)

Sources of carbohydrates

Sugars, starches and unavailable carbohydrates are found only in plant foods.

Sugar is extracted commercially from beet and cane. It is added to many foods and drinks, puddings, cakes, confectionery, preserves, ice-cream, fruit drinks and cola.

Starch is stored in the seeds and roots of many cultivated plants and provides a major part of man's food energy. Starch is in cereals including wheat, rice and maize; in cereal products such as bread, pasta and flour (puddings, cakes, pastry); in breakfast cereals, and in some vegetables, e.g. potatoes, peas.

Unavailable carbohydrates are present in natural, unrefined plant foods or whole foods. They are in breakfast cereals and flours made from the whole grain (i.e. containing bran), in wholemeal bread, potatoes and other vegetables, and in pulses, nuts and fruit.

**Functions of carbohydrates**

1. Sugars and starches provide energy (16 kJ/g) to keep the body alive and for activity. Protein can be 'burnt' for energy but this is wasteful. If carbohydrate and protein are eaten at the same meal, then the carbohydrate is used for energy thus sparing the protein for its primary task of growth and renewal. Sugars and starches can be changed into body fat as a reserve of energy for future use. Some carbohydrate should be eaten in order that fats in the body can be fully oxidised, otherwise headaches and nausea may result.
2. Cellulose, or dietary fibre, is necessary to aid peristalsis (movement of the digestive tract), and the regular elimination of waste materials. The fibre is able to hold water and so keep the faeces soft and bulky, thus preventing constipation.

**Requirements**

It is possible to exist without carbohydrates, e.g. the traditional Eskimo diet, but most people eat some plant food containing carbohydrates. In an average mixed diet about 50% of our energy comes from carbohydrates.

What is much more important to most of us is to avoid eating too much sugar and starch, thus becoming overweight. We should have enough each day to maintain our correct body weight but our appetite is not always a good judge of this! Too much sugar eaten in snacks between meals causes tooth decay, and there are other health hazards possibly associated with sugar. For good health, most of our carbohydrate should come from whole foods such as whole cereals and wholemeal bread, fruits, and vegetables including potatoes. These foods contain starch and cellulose with B vitamins and very little sugar. Cakes, ice-cream and sweet drinks are fun foods which we can have for special occasions.

**Behaviour of carbohydrates**

Sugars dissolve in water and taste sweet. A strong concentration of sugar acts as a preservative by reducing water activity. Sugars caramelise on heating. Some sugars react with protein to give a brown colour called the Maillard reaction. (See page 4.)

Starches do not dissolve in cold water and resist enzyme activity when uncooked. When heated in the presence of water, starch grains swell and, at about 100°C, gelatinise. The thickening of sauces is caused by the gelatinisation of starch. Dry heat causes starch to turn brown. This is probably caused by pyro-dextrins and can be seen in toast.

Cellulose softens in hot water. This makes it easier to chew and swallow but does not make it digestible. Pectin in cell walls dissolves in hot water. This contributes to the softening of vegetables and fruit when cooking. Pectin forms a gel with acid, sugar and water and is the thickening agent in jam.

(See page 23 for details of the digestion and metabolism of carbohydrates.)

## Fats

Nature of fats

Fats are nutrients composed of carbon, hydrogen and oxygen, with a lower proportion of oxygen than in carbohydrates. A great variety of fats and oils occur in animals and plants and are used in our diet. (Oils are fats which are liquid at room temperature.) Chemically, fats are all very similar, consisting of glycerol combined with three fatty acids called tri-glycerides:

—— Fatty acid 1
Glycerol —— Fatty acid 2
—— Fatty acid 3

The three fatty acids may be the same or any of a dozen or so different ones and this variation produces the wide variety of fats and oils found in nature. Fats and oils are mixtures of different tri-glycerides.

Some fatty acids are called saturated because, in their chemical structure, they have all the hydrogen atoms they can hold. Other fatty acids have some hydrogen atoms missing, – they are called unsaturated. If several hydrogen atoms are missing, they are called polyunsaturated fatty acids.

The proportion of saturated and unsaturated fatty acids in any fat determines whether it is an oil or a fat, soft or hard, e.g. suet contains the saturated palmitic and stearic acids; maize oil contains the unsaturated linoleic acid. Generally, fats from animals contain more saturated fatty acids and are hard fats. Fats from plants and fish contain unsaturated fatty acids and are liquid fats or oils. Some margarines are specially made with a high proportion of polyunsaturated fatty acids.

Source of fats

*Saturated fats*: in butter, cream, milk, cheese, fatty meat, suet, egg yolks and hard margarine.
*Unsaturated fats*: in most cooking oils, e.g. maize, soya, sunflower and olive oil; in nuts, polyunsaturated margarines; oily fish, e.g. herrings, mackerel, sardines and salmon.

Invisible fat is in protein foods such as meat, cheese, and milk; and in made-up foods such as cakes, pastries, confectionery and ice-cream. Visible fat is added during cooking, e.g. frying, and is served with carbohydrate foods, e.g. bread with butter.

One-third of the fats we eat are refined, i.e. they are extracted from the natural foods and used in a concentrated form, e.g. butter and margarine.

Functions of fats

1. Fats supply the body with a concentrated source of energy (37 kJ/g).
2. Fat is stored in the body as a reserve of fuel in layers under the skin. This also conserves body heat.
3. Some fats carry the fat-soluble vitamins A, D, E, and K.
4. Fats supply the essential fatty acids needed by the body.
5. Fats make the diet palatable and satisfying. They have a high satiety value as they are digested slowly.

Requirements

From 25%–30% of our energy intake should be in the form of fat. Much less than this may make the diet unpalatable but it would still supply all that the body requires. Above 40% would probably lead to obesity and maybe to coronary heart disease, depending on other factors. It is probably advisable to restrict the intake of butter, cream, fat meat and fried foods which contain large amounts of saturated fats. Instead choose chicken, fish or lean meat and foods fried in oil. However, the best advice is moderation in all things.

Behaviour of fats

Fats are solid at low temperatures and melt when heated. If heating continues, fats smoke and decompose into fatty acids and glycerol. Acrolein forms from the glycerol giving burnt fat a bitter taste. Fat does not boil but the vapours can catch alight easily if overheating occurs.

Fats do not dissolve in water. If they are mixed vigorously with water they can form an emulsion. The emulsion is stabilised by an emulsifier, e.g. egg proteins in mayonnaise.

Fats can be spoilt by rancidity. Oxidative rancidity is most common. Unsaturated fatty acids react with oxygen and produce substances that have an unpleasant taste and smell. They produce a tingling sensation in the mouth. Anti-oxidants are added to many processed foods to prevent rancidity.

Hydrolytic rancidity is caused by fatty acids splitting from the glycerol. The unpleasant taste and smell are characteristic of each fatty acid, e.g. butyric acid in rancid butter. This rancidity occurs in the presence of water when enzymes or micro-organisms are present.

(See page 23 for details of the digestion and metabolism of fats.)

## Minerals

Nature of minerals

Minerals in food are those elements other than carbon, hydrogen, oxygen and nitrogen. They are necessary to the body and must be supplied by food. They are the elements that are found in the ash after the body is cremated and they make up about 4% of the total body weight.

The major minerals are calcium, phosphorus, sulphur, potassium, sodium, chlorine, magnesium and iron. These are needed in the greatest amount in the diet or are present in the largest amounts in the body.

Other minerals, or trace elements, are essential but in much smaller quantities; they include fluorine, iodine, zinc and copper. Most elements are easily obtained from a varied diet and deficiencies seldom occur. However, the body requirements for some elements may at times be increased and then it is especially important that the diet supplies sufficient in a form which the body can easily absorb.

General functions of minerals

1. To build up strong bones and teeth, e.g. calcium, phosphorus, magnesium.
2. To help make body cells, e.g. iron, sulphur, phosphorus, potassium.
3. To keep the composition of all body fluids correct, e.g. sodium, chlorine.
4. For the proper functioning of the enzyme systems of the body, especially in the release and use of energy, e.g. iron, phosphorus and some trace elements.

Iron

Iron is needed to make haemoglobin, the red colour in blood, which is essential for the transport of oxygen. Only small amounts are needed in the diet because, once absorbed, it can be reused in the body to make new haemoglobin. Losses occur through bleeding and through the small amounts lost in the faeces; also through general wear and tear. If insufficient iron is obtained from food, poor health and anaemia will result. The patient will be pale, listless and become tired easily.

Everyone needs a basic supply of iron but in some circumstances extra is required. Women need more than men because of the monthly loss of blood. Rapid growth, e.g. during adolescence and in pregnancy, also increases the need for iron. Babies are born with a six-month supply of iron in their livers. At the weaning age, iron should be supplied by meat, liver, vegetables and egg yolk.

Sources of iron:
Meat, especially liver and kidney; bread and flour, (iron is added during manufacture); vegetables, especially potatoes, beans and green vegetables; egg yolks; dried fruit; corned beef; curry powder and cocoa powder.

If liver is eaten once a week, the iron is stored and can be used when necessary. Iron is not easily washed out of food during preparation and cooking. Some may be added from utensils and cooking water. Iron in red meat is attached to the haem protein and is best absorbed in this form.

Iron is not available to the body when combined with phytic acid or oxalic acid; so spinach, rhubarb and cereals must not be relied upon as the main source of iron, as they contain these acids.

Calcium

The functions of calcium:
1. The proper development and growth of bones and teeth – in combination with phosphorus and magnesium.
2. The contraction of muscles, nerve function and enzyme activity.
3. The normal clotting of blood.
The presence of vitamin D is necessary for the absorption of calcium.

Calcium is usually present in the diet in sufficient amounts. However, if vitamin D is missing, then too little calcium is absorbed. In young children this results in rickets (page 12); in adults the bones and teeth may become decalcified.

All adults need a basic supply of calcium to replace small daily losses. Extra is needed for growing children and adolescents. Expectant and nursing mothers also need extra amounts of calcium. If there is insufficient in their diets, it is withdrawn from their own bones and teeth.

Milk, skimmed milk powder, evaporated milk and cheese are the best sources, as the protein and lactose aid absorption of the mineral. Cereals contain some calcium. In the UK it is added to white flour by the millers.

Canned fish, e.g. salmon and sardines, is a good source, provided that the soft bones are eaten.

Green vegetables contain some calcium and will acquire more if boiled in hard water. Hard water is a significant source of calcium.

Calcium is not lost or destroyed during food preparation and cooking. Phytic acid and oxalic acid interfere with absorption, thus making the calcium unavailable.

**Phosphorus**

Phosphorus is essential for the release of energy from nutrients. It forms bones and teeth in conjunction with calcium and it helps to regulate the acidity of body fluids.

It is widely available, especially in protein-rich foods, and deficiency is unknown.

**Sodium and chlorine**

The body needs both these elements and they are supplied by sodium chloride or common salt. All body fluids contain salt, which helps to maintain the correct water balance in the body. If an excess of salt is taken, it is excreted in the urine. If too little is taken, muscular cramps result. If much salt is lost in excessive sweating in hot conditions, then extra is needed, e.g. in soup or as tablets.

**Potassium**

Potassium is needed to maintain the composition of body cells. It is widely available in meat, milk, fruits and vegetables.

**Iodine**

Iodine is needed to form hormones in the thyroid gland. It is found in seafoods and is added to table salt in the U.K. Deficiency causes goitre, the thyroid gland in the neck becoming enlarged.

**Fluorine**

Bones and teeth contain fluorine and it is important in preventing tooth decay. The surface enamel of teeth is strengthened by fluorine. Fluorine is found naturally in water supplies in some areas; in others it is sometimes added at the rate of one part per million.

**Summary table of minerals**

| *Minerals* | *Why they are needed* | *Where they are found* |
|---|---|---|
| Calcium | To build strong bones and teeth<br>To help working of muscles<br>To help blood clot on wounds | Milk, cheese, added to flour and bread, canned fish, green vegetables |
| Iron | To make haemoglobin in the blood | Liver, meat, added to flour and bread, egg yolk, pulses, potatoes, dried fruit |
| Phosphorus | With calcium to form bones and teeth. For release of energy from nutrients. To regulate acidity of body fluids | Cheese, eggs, meat and fish, added to processed foods |
| Sodium | To regulate the composition of body fluids | Salt and all salted foods |
| Potassium | To regulate the working of body cells | Fruit and vegetables |
| Iodine | For thyroid hormones | Iodised salt, seafoods, drinking water |
| Fluorine | To strengthen teeth | Drinking water, tea, seafoods |

## Vitamins

Nature of vitamins

Vitamins are substances, present in foods in very minute quantities, which are essential for growth and for maintaining health. When they were first discovered, their chemical nature was not known and they were named alphabetically. Some were found mainly in fatty foods and were named the fat-soluble vitamins (vitamins A, D, E and K). Others were water-soluble (vitamins of the B group and C). It has been found that there is sometimes more than one chemical with the same vitamin activity.

Retinol (vitamin A)

The functions of retinol:
1. It is essential for vision in dim light. Deficiency causes night blindness.
2. It is necessary for healthy skin and moist surface tissues, e.g. in the eyes and in the lungs, so helping to protect against infection. Deficiency causes the cornea of the eye to become dry, thickened and opaque, so producing a different kind of blindness called xerophthalmia.
3. It is necessary for growth of children. Deficiency is frequently associated with protein-energy malnutrition.

Two forms of vitamin A exist in food:
1. Retinol, which is found only in animal fats or fatty foods, e.g. fish liver oils, liver, kidney, egg yolk, milk and cheese, butter, margarine (added in manufacture).
2. Carotenes, a group of orange pigments, found in fruits and

vegetables, which can be partly converted to retinol by the body. It occurs in carrots, spinach; watercress, cabbage, apricots. Vitamin A in dairy foods is formed by cows from carotene in the grass eaten, so there is more in summer milk and butter.

As vitamin A is not soluble in water it is not easily lost from food during preparation and cooking. It is destroyed by heat only at high temperatures, e.g. by frying.

Retinol is stored in the liver, so if we eat more than our daily requirements, the extra can be kept until needed. Concentrated forms of retinol, e.g. capsules, should not be taken in excessive amounts as it accumulates in the liver.

Calciferol (vitamin D)

Vitamin D with calcium and phosphorus is necessary for building strong bones and teeth. It is called the calcifying vitamin as it helps in absorbing the calcium from the intestines and in laying down calcium phosphate in bones and teeth.

Shortage of vitamin D causes rickets in children, i.e. if young bones do not contain enough calcium they will be soft and become unable to support a child's weight. This shows as bandy legs or knock-knees. In adolescents and women, lack of vitamin D can cause decalcification of the bones. Lack of vitamin D causes calcium deficiency.

Sources of calciferol:
1. Sunlight acts on a substance in the skin and produces calciferol in our bodies.
2. Some fatty foods contain vitamin D: oily fish, e.g. mackerel, herring, sardines, salmon, tuna; it is added to margarine and evaporated milk during manufacture; eggs, milk, cheese, butter.

Sunshine is an important source for most people and vitamin D created in this way can be stored in the liver. Housebound people or those preferring to wear enveloping clothing need to ensure that their food contains sufficient vitamin D, as do children and pregnant women whose requirements are high. Vitamin D is not destroyed during normal cooking processes. Like retinol, calciferol is stored in the liver.

Vitamin E

This vitamin occurs widely in foods and is stored in the body, so deficiency is unlikely. The richest sources are vegetable oils, cereal products and eggs.

Vitamin K

This vitamin occurs in green, leafy vegetables in association with vitamins A and C. It is also synthesised by bacteria in the large intestine. It is one of the substances necessary for the clotting of blood and is known as the coagulation vitamin.

*Vitamin B group*

The B vitamins are all different chemical substances although they are all water-soluble and tend to occur in the same foods. They are necessary for the efficient working of the enzyme systems for the release of energy.

**Thiamin**

Thiamin or vitamin $B_1$, is necessary for the release of energy from carbohydrates. The amount required is related to the energy intake.

A slight deficiency leads to a slowing down in the growth of children. It causes loss of appetite, fatigue, digestive disorders and irritability. A diet of carbohydrate foods without thiamin, e.g. polished rice, eaten over a long period produces the disease beri-beri.

It is widely distributed in natural, whole plant and animal foods. It can be lost during refining or processing, e.g. it is found in whole, brown rice but the removal of the bran reduces the thiamin. There is no thiamin in fats and sugar. Good sources of thiamin are: pork and other meats; eggs; vegetables; fruit; whole grain and fortified cereals. In the UK, white flour and bread are fortified with thiamin.

**Riboflavin**

Riboflavin or vitamin $B_2$, is essential for the release of energy from nutrients. Deficiency produces no specific disease; the reason for this is a mystery. Minor signs of deficiency are a check in the growth of children, sores in the corners of the mouth and unhealthy skin.

It is widely distributed in natural foods, especially animal foods. Milk is the single most important source in the UK. Liver and eggs are also good sources.

**Nicotinic acid**

This is needed for the release of energy in the oxidation of nutrients. Minor signs of deficiency include a check in the growth of children, digestive disorders and reddened, scaly skin where exposed to the light. In extreme cases pellagra results, (the disease of the three D's – dermatitis, diarrhoea and dementia).

Sources of nicotinic acid:
1. The amino acid tryptophan can be converted to nicotinic acid in the body. Tryptophan occurs in most protein-rich foods, so they are a good source of this vitamin.
2. Nicotinic acid occurs in most natural foods such as meat, vegetables and milk. In the UK it is added to flour, thus bread is a good source.

**How cooking affects B group vitamins**

All B vitamins may be dissolved out of food into cooking water. Some are destroyed in alkaline conditions. The addition of sodium bicarbonate, baking powder or sulphur dioxide will reduce the thiamin and riboflavin content of foods. Yeast is a raising agent which is a good source of B vitamins, is not alkaline and so does not destroy the vitamins. B vitamins are partly destroyed at the high temperatures reached in baking, frying and canning. Riboflavin is destroyed by ultra-violet light, so milk should not be left on the doorstep but kept in a dark place.

**Ascorbic acid (vitamin C)**

This is needed for the formation and maintenance of the 'cement', or ground substance, which joins cells together to make tissues in all parts of the body, particularly in connective tissue, blood capillaries, bones and teeth. It is necessary for growth in children, for healing of wounds and for the prevention of scurvy. Minor deficiency will produce a check in the growth of children, bleeding, particularly in the gums, and the slow healing of wounds and fractures. Prolonged deficiency causes scurvy in which the gums bleed, teeth fall out, joints swell, wounds fail to heal and death results. This disease was once common among sailors on long voyages when fresh fruit and vegetables were not available. It was a contributing cause of the failure of Scott's Antarctic expedition.

Ascorbic acid is found in varying amounts in fruits and vegetables. Good sources are: blackcurrants, strawberries, citrus fruits, Brussels sprouts, cabbage, cauliflower, broccoli and new potatoes. There is little vitamin C in dried vegetables. Potatoes are an important source. They are cheap, easily available and, eaten regularly in large amounts, they contribute useful amounts of vitamin C to the diet. The vitamin content decreases when they are stored during the winter.

**Conservation of ascorbic acid**

Vitamin C is easily lost from food because:
1. It is soluble in water.
2. It is destroyed by air (oxidation).

The enzyme oxidase, heat, alkali and metals such as iron and copper will all accelerate the destruction of vitamin C.

Acid, as found in fruit; sulphur dioxide, used as a preservative; low temperatures, as in a refrigerator or freezer; will help to preserve vitamin C.

Therefore, to conserve vitamin C:
1. Prepare vegetables just before cooking. Do not soak them in water but wash them briefly under a running tap. When cooking, use only a little water in a covered pan, and use this water in gravy or soup.
2. Cook vegetables for as short a time as possible and serve at once. Do not keep them warm for a long period.
3. Any foods exposed to air for a long time lose vitamin C. Mashed vegetables, e.g. potatoes, lose vitamin C. Avoid using alkaline bicarbonate of soda when cooking green vegetables.
4. Cells damaged by wilting, bruising, cutting and grating release the enzyme oxidase which destroys vitamin C. This enzyme is destroyed by boiling water. Therefore, vegetables should be cut immediately prior to cooking and placed in boiling water. Acid salad dressing also stops enzyme activity and conserves vitamin C.

**Metabolism of vitamins**

Vitamins require no digestion. The water-soluble vitamins B and C are absorbed both in the stomach and the small intestine. They are used where required and any excess is excreted in the urine; they cannot be stored in the body. The fat-soluble vitamins A and D are also absorbed in the small intestine. They cannot be excreted as they are not water-soluble, so any excess is stored in the liver for use when required. To ensure a good supply of vitamins:

1. Eat as great a variety of foods as possible. Eat dairy foods for vitamins A, $B_2$ and D; fresh fruit and vegetables for vitamins A and C; meat and bread for vitamins B.
2. Eat some raw foods, e.g. fruits and salads. Avoid too much refined and processed foods, e.g. fats and sugar.
3. Cook food with care to retain full vitamin content.
4. Give supplementary sources to babies, infants, expectant mothers and those confined to institutions.

**Summary table of vitamins**

| *Name* | *Function* | *Sources* | *Result of deficiency* |
|---|---|---|---|
| A retinol, carotenes | Growth, eyesight, resistance to infection, healthy skin | Margarine, oily fish, green vegetables, carrots | Night blindness, rough skin, infections, xerophthalmia |
| B thiamin, riboflavin, nicotinic acid | Growth, release of energy from nutrients | Natural foods, bread, meat, milk, yeast products | Slow growth, fatigue, irritability, beri-beri (thiamin), pellegra (nicotinic acid) |
| C ascorbic acid | Growth, connective tissue, healing | Blackcurrants, oranges and lemons, new potatoes, cabbage and sprouts | Slow healing, gums bleed, irritability, scurvy |
| D calciferol | Absorption of calcium for bones and teeth | Sunshine, oily fish, margarine, butter | Rickets, loss of muscle tone, decalcified bones and teeth |

## Water

Functions of water

Water is vital to life. The body's need for water is second only to its need for air.

Water is needed for:

1. Building the body tissues. (About three-quarters of the body, by weight, is water.)
2. All the complex chemical changes which take place in the body.
3. The removal of waste substances by the kidneys, i.e. in urine.
4. The regulation of body temperature by the sweat glands.
5. As the solvent for the digestion, absorption and metabolism of food.
6. As the chief constituent of all body fluids, e.g. blood, digestive juices, mucus.

Requirements

The body must be kept in a state of 'water balance', i.e. we must replace the water lost by the kidneys as urine, the skin as sweat and the lungs as water vapour.

This water is replaced by:
1. Water in the fluids we drink. (The average amount we need to drink is about one-and-a-half litres per day.)
2. Water in so-called 'solid' foods.
3. Water we make when nutrients are burnt or oxidised in the tissues, i.e. metabolic water.

Absorption and excretion of water

About one-fifth of the water drunk is absorbed through the stomach walls, the rest through the walls of the small and large intestines. This enters the blood vessels and is taken to all parts of the body. Extra water as a drink will not make healthy people fat; the kidneys can excrete it all. However, if other nutrients such as sugar, fat or protein are present, they will add to the daily energy intake.

Dehydration may occur under certain conditions if sufficient water is not taken. Sweating, diarrhoea and vomiting cause extra loss of water. Babies need drinks of water or dilute fruit juice in hot weather as they can lose a lot of water by sweating. Milk is not always suitable as a drink because it may make the urine too concentrated.

**Dietary fibre**

Several materials, e.g. cellulose and pectin, are classed as dietary fibre; they are carbohydrates (see page 5). They are not digested by humans and so the energy they contain is unavailable, hence the alternative name of unavailable carbohydrates. Cellulose forms the cell walls of plants and the fibrous parts such as stems, seed coverings and skins. Pectin is found in the soft tissues of underipe fruit.

Functions of dietary fibre

Dietary fibre passes unchanged through the digestive tract. In the large intestine it holds water which keeps the waste food material soft and bulky. It stimulates peristalsis and this movement of the gut ensures regular elimination of the faeces, or waste material. If we do not have enough fibre in our diet, the small residue of waste material stays in the gut for too long; elimination is irregular. This is known as constipation. Other illnesses of people in western civilizations may be attributed to lack of fibre, although the evidence is not clear.

Sources of fibre

Cereals and flours, especially those including the bran, e.g. wholemeal flour and brown rice; potatoes; green, leafy vegetables; peas and beans; nuts and fruits.

It is lacking in refined and processed foods, e.g. fats, sugar, cakes, biscuits, puddings, ice-cream and white bread. It does not occur in animal foods like meat, fish, eggs, milk or cheese.

**Energy**

Forms of energy

Energy has many forms, e.g. solar (the sun's energy), chemical, mechanical and thermal (heat) energy. Energy is needed for life and in life we change energy from one form to another. Thus plants convert the sun's energy to chemical energy in carbohydrates, fats and proteins. If we eat these nutrients, we can convert their energy to mechanical energy for activity, chemical energy for active tissues and heat energy for body warmth.

**Joules**

The unit of energy is the joule. This is an expression of the energy expended when 1 kilogram (kg) is moved 1 meter (m) by a force of 1 newton (N). In food we are concerned with large amounts of energy so we use the kiloJoule ($kJ = 10^3 J$) and the megaJoule ($MJ = 10^6 J$). Formerly kilocalories were used ($1\ kcal \times 4.2 = 1\ kJ$).

**Release of energy from food**

The nutrients which supply the body with energy are carbohydrates, fats, proteins and alcohol. When these substances are eaten, they are digested and absorbed. Then the body metabolises them; chemical reactions take place which release the energy from the nutrients and make it available to the cells of the body.

Energy is released in a complicated series of steps, each controlled by an enzyme. Vitamins are needed for some of these changes to take place efficiently. The whole series of reactions can be summarised by:

$$\text{Glucose} + \text{Oxygen} \xrightarrow[\text{of B vitamins}]{\text{in the presence}} \text{Energy} + \text{Carbon dioxide} + \text{water}$$

Fatty acids, glycerol, alcohol and derivatives of protein are oxidised like glucose to produce energy. Glucose and oxygen are taken to every cell of the body in the blood; carbon dioxide and water are removed as waste products.

**Uses of energy**

1. For basal metabolism, i.e. to keep alive. Even when the body is at rest, energy is needed by all the tissues. It is required for the heart and circulation, for breathing and to maintain correct body temperature.
2. For physical activity, i.e. movement requires energy. Strenuous activity requires more energy than light activity.
3. For special purposes, e.g. growth, pregnancy and lactation.

**Requirements**

The daily energy requirement of any adult is that amount which maintains correct body weight. The energy intake must balance the energy output. This depends on:

1. *Body size and composition*: heavy people use more energy than lighter people and so men tend to need more food than women. Men have more lean muscle tissue than women and therefore use more energy.

2. *Age*: requirements are proportionately higher in growing children than in older people. Elderly people have reduced requirements because of reduced body size and activity.

3. *Physical activity*: during both work and leisure this is the most important factor affecting energy requirements. People can be

divided into three categories according to their occupations:

a) Sedentary workers, e.g. clerks, drivers, professional people.

b) Moderately active workers, e.g. most industrial workers, postmen, railwaymen.

c) Very active workers, e.g. miners at the coal face, some building labourers and army recruits.

Mechanisation has reduced the amount of labour and effort required in many types of work. Short bursts of activity do not use much energy; the activity must be maintained for long periods to affect the energy requirements.

Recommended daily intake of energy:

| | *Age* | *Occupational category* | *MJ* | *kcal* |
|---|---|---|---|---|
| Boys | 7–8 | — | 8.25 | 1980 |
| Girls | 7–8 | — | 8.0 | 1900 |
| Boys | 15–17 | — | 12.0 | 2880 |
| Girls | 15–17 | — | 9.0 | 2150 |
| Men | 35–64 | Sedentary | 10.0 | 2400 |
| Men | 35–64 | Very active | 14.0 | 3350 |
| Women | 18–54 | Most occupations | 9.0 | 2150 |
| Men | 75+ | Sedentary | 9.0 | 2150 |
| Women | 75+ | Sedentary | 7.0 | 1680 |

## Obesity

Obesity is the state in which an excess of body fat accumulates. If a person eats or drinks foods which provide more energy than he uses in his daily activity the excess nutrients will be converted to body fat. Any food containing protein, fat, carbohydrate or alcohol can be fattening. Foods rich in fat are concentrated sources of energy and watery foods contain little energy.

Causes of obesity include eating excessive amounts of attractive foods that are easily available, eating snack foods, e.g. sweets, crisps and sweetened drinks between meals, and excessive amounts of alcoholic drinks.

Some people do not grow fat because they are able to metabolise or 'burn up' all the food they eat, even if it is much more than they would normally eat. Some people grow fat easily because the body is unable to metabolise even small excesses of nutrients.

## Energy sources in food

Sources are: cereal products including bread, flour, cakes, pastries, biscuits and breakfast cereals; dairy foods such as milk, butter and cheese; meat; fats; sugar and preserves; potatoes. All these foods supply energy and have a place in a good mixed diet. If a high energy intake is required then bread and butter, milk, pastry and meats are good sources. If a low energy intake is required, it is best to avoid too much sugar and preserves, cakes, pastries and biscuits. The quality of these foods depends not only on the energy content but on the other nutrients that are present with the fat and carbohydrate, e.g. vitamins and minerals.

Energy values

1 g dietary carbohydrate provides 16 kJ or 3.75 kcal
1 g dietary fat provides 37 kJ or 9 kcal
1 g dietary protein provides 17 kJ or 4 kcal
1 g dietary alcohol provides 29 kJ or 7 kcal

Tables of food composition are available from which we find, for example, that 100 g bread contains:
7.8 g protein
1.7 g fat
49.7 g carbohydrate

Thus the energy content of 100 g bread will be:

| | | | |
|---|---|---|---|
| $7.8 \times 17$ | = | 132.6 | kJ from protein |
| $1.7 \times 37$ | = | 62.9 | kJ from fat |
| $49.7 \times 16$ | = | 795.2 | kJ from carbohydrate |
| Total | | 990.7 | |

This is better expressed as 991 kJ as values are approximate.

# 2 Digestion and absorption of food

*The alimentary canal    Processes of digestion    Digestion, absorption and metabolism of the nutrients*

Digestion is the process by which the food we eat is changed into simpler substances so that they can be absorbed into the bloodstream and used by the body to maintain life.

## The alimentary canal

Digestion takes place in the alimentary canal, which reaches from the mouth to the anus. By the time food reaches the anus, most of the useful components have been absorbed through the walls of the canal. The substances which change the food or 'break it down' are called digestive enzymes.

The alimentary canal consists of the following parts: mouth, oesophagus, stomach, small intestine (duodenum and ileum), large intestine (colon), rectum and anus.

The food is moved through the canal by a rippling movement of the muscles in the canal walls. This movement is known as peristalsis or peristaltic action. Sphincter muscles at the lower end of the stomach (the pyloric valve) and at the anus play important parts in this process.

The food components needing digestion are:

1. *Proteins*, which must be broken down into amino acids.
2. *Fats*, which must be broken down into fatty acids and glycerol.
3. *Carbohydrates*, which must be broken down into the simplest sugars – i.e. monosaccharides.

*Minerals, vitamins and water* can be used by the body without being changed by digestion.

## Processes of digestion

In the mouth

Food is chewed into small pieces by the teeth and moistened with saliva to prepare it for swallowing. Saliva is slightly alkaline. It contains the enzyme salivary amylase (ptyalin) which starts the digestion of cooked starch. Some of the polysaccharide starch is changed to the disaccharide maltose.

In the oesophagus

No digestion takes place – it is merely a passage to the stomach.

In the stomach

The stomach walls secrete gastric juice containing hydrochloric acid and enzymes. The acid kills bacteria in the food and provides the right acidity for the enzyme activity. The enzyme pepsin begins the digestion of protein to polypeptides. Rennin is

*The digestive system*

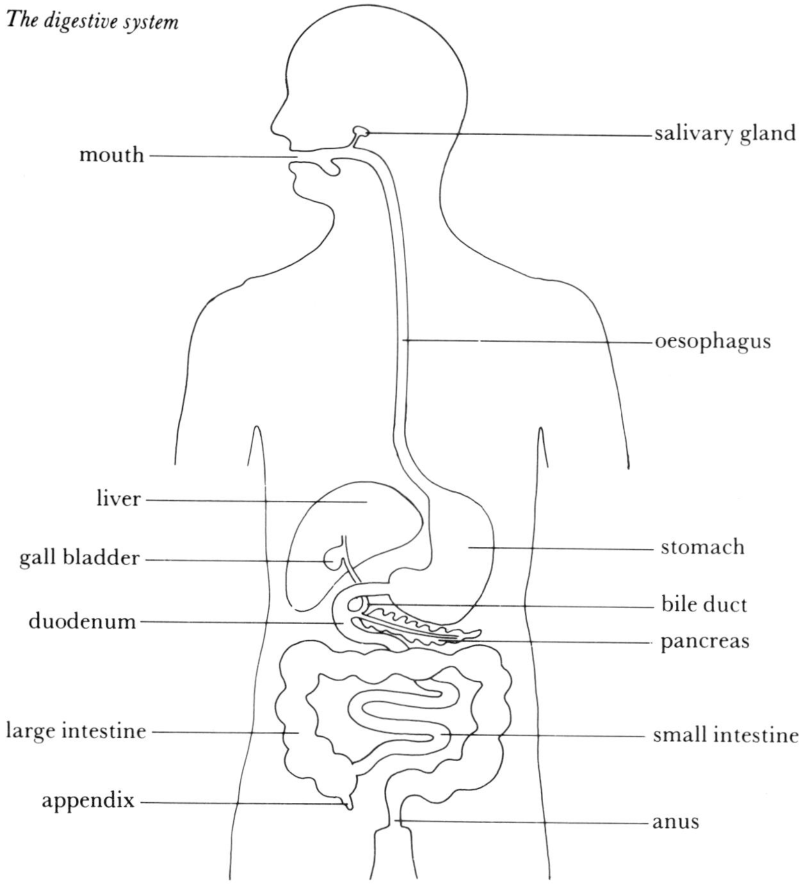


an enzyme which coagulates the milk protein caseinogen, forming casein curds. (This is important in infants, the solid curds staying in the stomach long enough for pepsin to begin their digestion.)

Different foods stay in the stomach for differing times. Fat stays longest and so is said to be satisfying. Fats are melted and the food is churned by the action of the muscular walls so that a semi-liquid chyme is formed.

In the small intestine (duodenum and ileum)

The first 25 cm or so of the small intestine is called the duodenum and this is the main area of digestion. In the duodenum three secretions mix with the semi-liquid chyme from the stomach:

1. The bile, made by the liver and stored in the gall bladder. This emulsifies fats and makes the chyme alkaline.
2. The pancreatic juice, from the pancreas, containing four enzymes that continue the breakdown of nutrients that was started in the stomach:

a) chymotrypsin and trypsin break down proteins into peptides.
b) lipase breaks down fats into fatty acids and glycerol.
c) pancreatic amylase completes the breakdown of starch into maltose.
3. The intestinal juice, from the walls of the small intestine, which contains peptidases which break down peptides into amino acids; maltase, lactase, and sucrase which break down the respective disaccharides into simple monosaccharides like glucose and fructose.

The soluble products of digestion are absorbed by the walls of the ileum or small intestine. Amino acids and simple sugars like glucose pass into the bloodstream and so to the liver. The fatty acids and glycerol reunite to form fat in the lacteals (lymph system) and enter the bloodstream later. Minerals, vitamins and water are unaffected by digestion and are absorbed.

The small intestine is long and the walls are folded and have many small projections known as villi which greatly increase the surface area through which absorption can take place.

In the large intestine

Water is absorbed. The undigested food is mainly fibre or cellulose from plants. This retains some water, increases the bulk of the waste material and stimulates the movement of the residues through the canal. Bacteria produce vitamins B and K. In the rectum, the 'waste food' is collected as faeces and then passed out of the body through the anus.

**Digestion, absorption and metabolism of the nutrients**

Proteins, fats and carbohydrates in food must be broken down by digestive enzymes into simple, soluble substances before they can be absorbed by the body. All these complex nutrients are made of smaller units and to split them the digestive enzymes introduce molecules of water, a process known as hydrolysis.

Digestion of proteins

*In the mouth*: no digestion.
*In the stomach*: digestion is started by the enzyme pepsin, in the presence of hydrochloric acid, which breaks down the protein into smaller chains of amino acids known as polypeptides. The enzyme rennin clots the casein of milk.
*In the duodenum*: trypsin and chymotrypsin from the pancreas continue to break down protein and polypeptides into peptides. Peptidases, a mixture of similar enzymes from the wall of the small intestine, finally complete the breakdown of peptides into amino acids.
*In the small intestine*: the amino acids are absorbed through the walls and enter the bloodstream.

Metabolism of amino acids

In the bloodstream, most of the amino acids are reformed into new, complex protein chains. The remainder are deaminated and oxidised to produce energy. Amino acids cannot be stored in the body for later use.

Digestion of carbohydrates

*In the mouth*: no digestion of sugars. Digestion of starch begins; it is hydrolysed, or split, by salivary amylase (ptyalin) and partly broken down into maltose.
*In the stomach*: no digestion of sugars or starches.
*In the duodenum*: starch is further broken down by pancreatic amylase into maltose units.
*In the small intestine*: monosaccharides (simple sugars) are absorbed. (They need no digestion.) Disaccharides are broken down into monosaccharides as follows: sucrose is split by sucrase into glucose and fructose; lactose (milk sugar) is split by lactase into glucose and galactose. The maltose formed by the digestion of starch, is split by maltase into glucose. These simple sugars are absorbed through the walls of the small intestine and pass into the bloodstream.

Metabolism of simple sugars

The glucose in the blood is passed to all body cells to be oxidised or 'burnt' for energy (See page 17). If there is too much glucose in the blood the liver changes some of it to glycogen and some to fat, which it stores as a reserve of energy. Glycogen is a polysaccharide which is stored in the liver and muscles. Fat is stored in adipose tissue.

Digestion of fats

*In the mouth*: no digestion.
*In the stomach*: no digestion but the fats are melted. Fats stay in the stomach for 2–4 hours, giving a satisfied feeling.
*In the duodenum*: the melted fats are emulsified by the bile from the liver and the chyme is made alkaline. The enzyme lipase, from the pancreatic juice, splits the fats into fatty acids and glycerol.
*In the small intestine*: the above products are absorbed through the intestinal walls into the lymphatic system and thence into the bloodstream.

Metabolism of fats

The body builds up its own fats from the absorbed food fats. They can then be oxidised in the tissues when energy is needed. Fats should be eaten with carbohydrates or they will be incompletely burnt and the resulting substances can cause sickness and headaches (ketosis).

Vitamins
Minerals
Water
Fibre

Vitamins, minerals and water need no digestion. They are mainly absorbed by the walls of the small intestine and pass into the bloodstream. Liquid, when swallowed alone, is absorbed by the walls of the stomach and intestines. Dietary fibre is not digested or absorbed but passes right through the alimentary canal and then out of the body.

**Summary of digestion**

| *Site* | *Nutrient* | *Enzyme* | *Product of Digestion* |
|---|---|---|---|
| Mouth | Starch | Salivary amylase | Maltose |
| Stomach | Milk protein | Rennin | Casein curds |
| | Protein | Pepsin | Polypeptides |
| Duodenum | Fats | (None) | Emulsified fats |
| | Protein | Chymotrypsin and trypsin | Peptides |
| | Starch | Pancreatic amylase | Maltose |
| | Fats | Lipase | Fatty acids and glycerol |
| Small intestine | Peptides | Peptidases | Amino acids |
| | Maltose | Maltase | Glucose |
| | Lactose | Lactase | Glucose and galactose |
| | Sucrose | Sucrase | Glucose and fructose |

# 3 Animal foods which provide protein

*Meat, fish, eggs, milk and cheese   Their composition, structure and value in the diet   Action of cooking on these foods   How to choose them*

## Meat

The term meat includes the flesh of slaughtered animals and birds, e.g. cattle, pigs, sheep, chickens, ducks.

Classification of meat

1. Muscular cuts from the muscles which cover the skeleton.
*White meat*: e.g. veal, rabbit, chicken, is of looser texture than red meat and contains less fat and connective tissue.
*Red meat*: e.g. beef, pork, lamb has more flavour than white meat. There is little difference between the nutritive values of the two types.
2. *Offal*: the term applied to organs of the animal's body, e.g. liver, kidney, tripe. They differ in structure according to the individual functions.

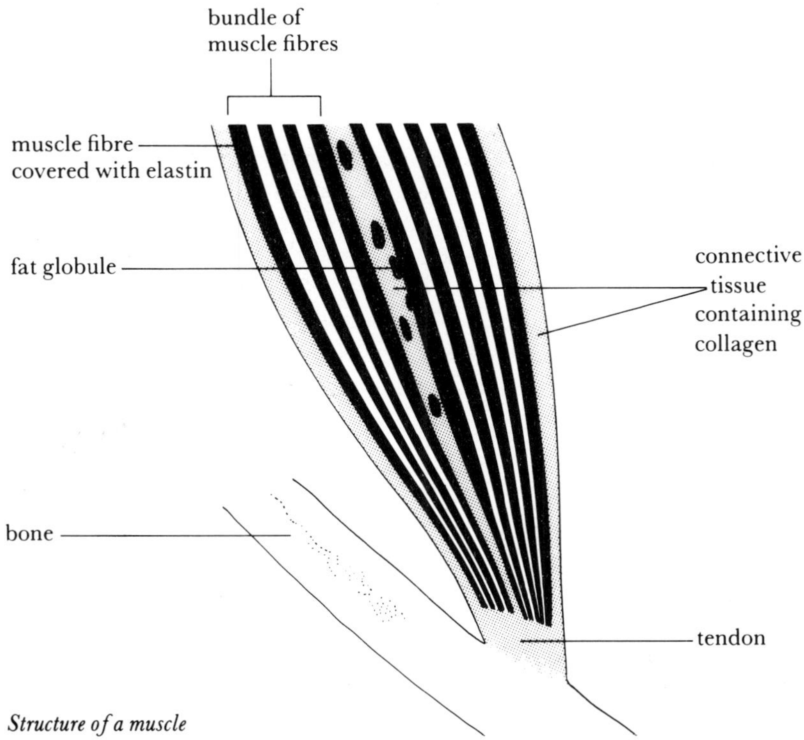


*Structure of a muscle*

Structure of meat

Lean meat consists of bundles of muscle fibres which lie side by side, held together by connective tissue. The bundles are joined to the bones by tendons. Each fibre is made up of cells containing the proteins myosin and actin and a watery solution of mineral salts, vitamins and extractives. These extractives give the flavour to the meat. The walls of the fibres are composed of the protein elastin, and the connective tissue contains the protein collagen. Fat cells ('invisible' fat) are found in the connective tissue between the fibres. There are also special fat deposits ('visible' fat) in various parts of the animal's body, e.g. under the skin and around the internal organs.

Composition of meat

Lean meat consists of proteins such as myosin, actin and globulin. These provide all the essential amino acids and so are of high biological value.

Fat is present in varying amounts.

The minerals iron, potassium and phosphorus are found in all meat, especially in liver and kidney.

All the vitamins of the B complex are present in lean meats and vitamin A occurs in liver.

The coarser lean cuts of meat are equal in food value to prime cuts but they require slow, moist cooking. Offal is a valuable addition to the diet. Liver is an excellent source of protein, vitamins A and B and iron. (Cook liver briefly and gently to render it easily digestible.) Kidney and heart are good sources of protein and iron. Brain, tripe and sweetbreads are also good sources of protein and are very easily digested.

Meat does not contain carbohydrate, calcium or vitamin C and should be served with foods supplying these nutrients.

Tenderness of meat

Meat must be hung for some time after it is slaughtered. During hanging certain acids develop which tenderise the fibres and the connective tissue. Young animals produce more tender meat than old animals because they have short, fine meat fibres and little connective tissue or gristle. Tender cuts of meat are usually from that part of the animal which had little muscular movement when it was alive. The hind-quarter of the carcass contains more of the tender cuts than the fore-quarter, hence the difference in price when bulk-buying for a freezer.

| *Tender meat* | *Tough meat* |
|---|---|
| Well hung meat | Not properly hung meat |
| Young animals | Old animals |
| Hind-quarter of carcass | Fore-quarter of carcass |
| Little used muscles, e.g. fillet steak | Much used muscles, e.g. leg of beef |
| Little connective tissue | Much connective tissue |
| Short, fine muscle fibres | Long, coarse muscle fibres |

Effect of cooking on meat

Cooking improves flavour and appearance. Heating causes the extractives to be squeezed out of the fibres and dry heat, in particular, causes these to brown on the surface.

Cooking destroys harmful parasites and bacteria so the meat

is safe to eat. Enzymes in the meat are inactivated, thus the meat can be kept longer. If frozen meat is not completely thawed before cooking, it may be tough and there is a risk of food poisoning. This is especially so in chicken, where the centre of the carcass may be infected with bacteria that are not destroyed if the meat does not reach a sufficiently high temperature whilst cooking.

The proteins of the muscle fibres coagulate and the meat becomes firm. If cooking is continued the fibres shrink and the juice is squeezed out, so losing some of the succulence.

In moist cooking conditions, the connective tissue is softened as the protein collagen is changed to gelatin. Gelatin dissolves in the liquid and muscle fibres fall apart, the meat becoming tender and digestible.

The red colour, myoglobin, in the meat changes to the brown substance, metmyoglobin.

The fat in meat melts and runs out. Some B vitamins are lost in meat drippings but are present in the gravy.

### Digestibility of meat

This depends on the amount of fat and connective tissue present, and on the coarseness of the muscle fibres. During moist cooking conditions collagen in connective tissue is changed to gelatin. This allows digestive enzymes to reach the meat fibres and so improves digestibility. A high fat content slows down the rate at which enzymes can digest the protein.

The extractives of cooked meat have a stimulating effect on the flow of gastric juice, thus aiding digestion.

### Choosing meat

1. All lean meat must be firm and elastic to touch.
2. There must be no strong smell.
3. Meat must be moist but not wet.
4. Any fluid must be watery but not sticky.
5. *Beef*: the lean is dark red, the fat is firm and yellow.
   *Lamb*: the lean is dull red, the fat is hard and white.
   *Pork*: the lean is pale pink, the fat is soft and white.
   *Bacon*: the lean is pink, the fat is white.
   *Veal*: the lean is pale and soft and there is very little fat.
   *Chicken*: plump with a pliable breast bone.

For roasting, grilling and frying, the more expensive cuts which have shorter fibres and less connective tissue are required. For boiling, stewing and braising, the cheaper cuts may be used, as these can be made tender by careful cooking.

### Meat storage

Food poisoning can be caused by careless handling and poor storage of meat products. There is danger of contamination from: (a) parasites; (b) harmful bacteria; (c) toxins formed by bacteria.

The storage times given below are only meant as a rough guide. They will depend on storage conditions before purchase which are not always known, so commonsense should prevail; if there is any doubt whatsoever about freshness, the meat should not be used. The sense of smell is usually the most accurate guide to the freshness of meat. Stale, raw meat quickly develops a smell of ammonia or a putrid odour.

*Raw meat*: this should first be wiped with a clean, damp cloth. Keep cool, clean and covered (in a refrigerator), *or* hang in a cool airy place, protected from flies, *or* salt by immersing in brine or by rubbing in dry salt. It should not be kept for longer than 1–2 days in a cool larder, or 2–4 days in a refrigerator. Raw meat can contain food poisoning bacteria which may infect other foods, so contact between raw and cooked meats must be avoided. Bacteria multiply rapidly in cooked meat so food poisoning could occur. Chopping boards and knives, and the drip from thawing meat are possible sources of contamination.

*Frozen meat*: this should be stored in a freezer at −18°C. When thawing ready for use, frozen meat should be unwrapped and put on a plate, loosely covered and left in a cool place to thaw slowly. Do not refreeze thawed meat, as harmful bacteria may have started to multiply.

*Offal*: place in a non-airtight container or cover loosely and keep very cool. Offal should not be kept for longer than one day in a cool larder, or 1–2 days in a refrigerator, as it is particularly liable to rapid spoilage.

*Cooked meat*: cool quickly, store covered in a cool place. It should keep 1–2 days in a cool place and 3–4 days in a refrigerator.

*Bacon*: This should be wrapped loosely in greaseproof paper and kept in a covered container. It will keep 3–4 days in a cool larder or up to 7 days in a refrigerator.

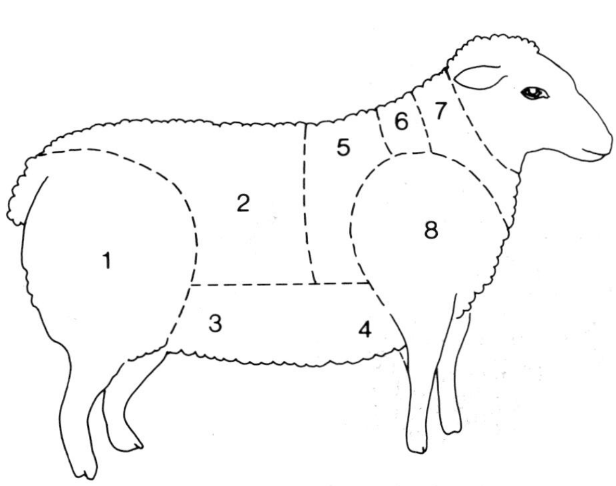


*Cuts of lamb, and how to cook them*

1 Leg to roast or boil
2 Loin to roast, or to cut in chops to grill or fry
3 Flank to stew
4 Breast to stew
5 Best end of neck to roast or to cut into cutlets to grill or fry
6 Middle neck to stew
7 Scrag end of neck to stew
8 Shoulder to roast

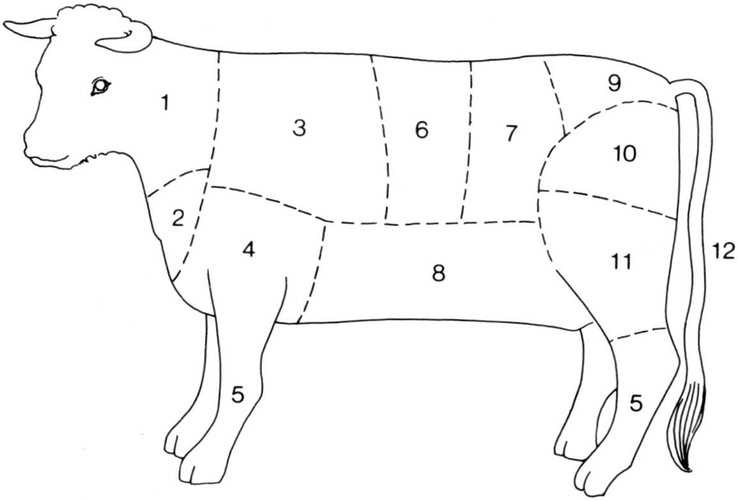


*Cuts of beef, and how to cook them*

1 Neck to stew
2 Clod to stew
3 Foreribs to roast
4 Brisket to boil, salt and boil, or slow roast
5 Shin to stew
6 Wing rib to roast
7 Sirloin to roast
8 Flank to salt and boil, or to stew
9 Rump and fillet to roast, grill or fry
10 Topside to roast
11 Silverside to boil, or to salt and boil
12 Oxtail to stew

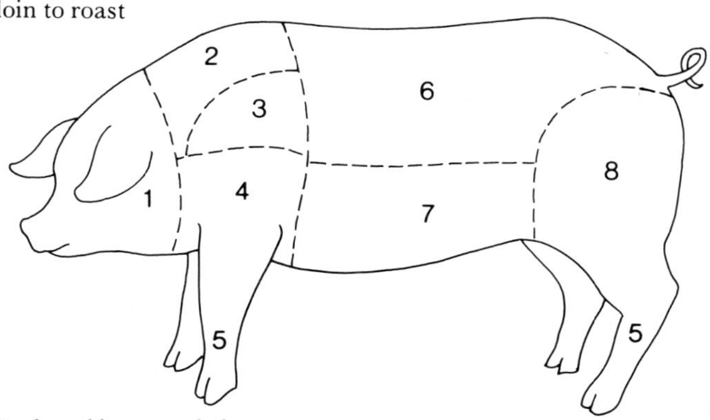


*Cuts of pork, and how to cook them*

1 Head to salt and boil, to make into brawn
2 Spare rib to roast, or to cut into chops to grill or fry
3 Blade to roast
4 Hand to roast or boil
5 Foot to stew for brawn or trotters
6 Loin to roast, or to cut into chops to grill or fry
7 Belly to boil, stew or pickle
8 Leg to roast or to salt and boil

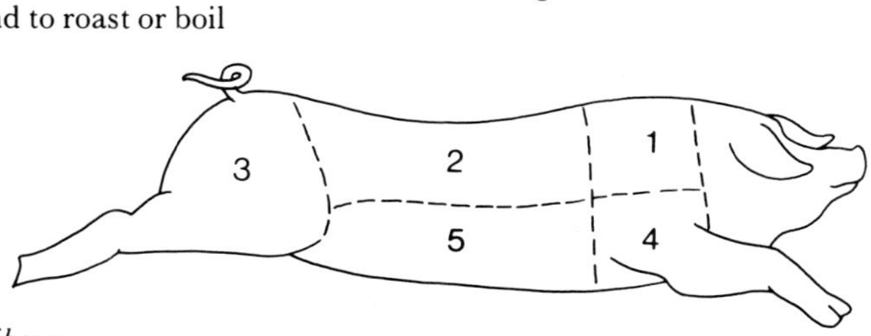


*Cuts of bacon*

1 Collar
2 Back
3 Gammon
4 Hock
5 Streaky

**Suitable cuts of meat for different methods of cooking**

| | *Lamb* | *Beef* | *Pork* | *Bacon* |
|---|---|---|---|---|
| Roasting | Loin, leg, shoulder | Sirloin, ribs | Loin, leg | Ham, after par-boiling |
| Grilling and frying | Loin-chops, cutlets | Fillet or rump steak | Loin-chops, spare-rib | Streaky or back rashers |
| Boiling | Sheep's head | Silverside | Belly | Hock, collar, gammon ham |
| Stewing | Scrag end of neck | Shin, chucksteak, oxtail | Belly, hand | |
| Braising | Heart | Brisket | | |

Meat production and processing

Meat is costly to produce and is therefore an expensive food. We need to choose and use meat economically not always expecting to have prime cuts. It is not possible, for example, to produce only lamb chops, the rest of the carcass must be used. Home Economists should be capable of preparing second quality cuts of meat in attractive and palatable ways.

The butchers and food manufacturers can also turn the tougher carcass meat into convenience foods. This saves the housewife time and trouble and provides an acceptable product at a reasonable price, e.g. sausages, pies, beefburgers, faggots, brawn and dehydrated re-formed meat. These products contain less lean meat than the equivalent weight of prime carcass meat. Most people in the UK eat more animal protein than they need, therefore the inclusion of convenience meat products in the diet does not adversely affect their level of nutrition.

## Fish

Classification of fish

1. *White fish*: these have all their fat stored in the liver, which is not usually eaten. White fish can be: a) round fish, e.g. whiting, cod; b) flat fish, e.g. plaice, sole, turbot.
2. *Oily fish*: these have the fat distributed through the flesh, which is, therefore, darker in colour, e.g. herring, mackerel, salmon, sardines.
3. *Shellfish*: these are protected by a hard external shell. They may be: a) crustaceans, e.g. crab, lobster, crayfish; b) molluscs (living inside a bi-valvular shell), e.g. cockles, mussels, oysters. Shellfish have their fat stored in the liver.

Structure of fish

The flesh consists of flakes made up of bundles of muscle fibres, shorter than those of meat. These are held together by small amounts of connective tissue containing collagen.

### Composition of fish

Fish contains protein of high biological value with useful amounts of B vitamins and minerals. Sea fish are a good source of the mineral elements iodine and fluorine. Canned fish are a rich source of calcium and phosphorus provided the softened bones are eaten. Oily fish contain unsaturated fats and the fat-soluble vitamins A and D. The livers of white fish such as cod and halibut are valuable sources of vitamins A and D, and oils extracted from these fish are used as medicinal supplements to the diet.

### Effect of cooking on fish

The muscle proteins coagulate on heating and the flesh becomes white and opaque. If fish is overcooked the proteins shrink, squeeze out liquid and the fish becomes dry. The collagen in connective tissue is easily changed to gelatin, the muscle fibres fall apart and the fish is tender to eat. Fat from oily fish melts and runs out. Fish needs only gentle cooking for a short time.

### Digestibility of fish

White fish is very easily digested as it contains no fat and little connective tissue. The flakes are, therefore, easily broken apart during cooking. This class of fish is very suitable for invalids and young children.

Oily fish is slightly more difficult to digest as the fat is distributed through the flesh.

Shellfish, such as crabs and lobsters, are difficult to digest as the fibres are long and tough.

### Uses of fish in meal planning

1. As a useful alternative to meat in main meals. Many oily fish such as herrings, sprats and mackerel are an inexpensive source of animal protein.
2. If suitably cooked, fish can be given to infants and invalids.
3. It can be used for snack meals, e.g. sardines on toast.
4. It can be served cold with salad.
5. Frozen fish and fish products can be used as convenience foods, e.g. fish fingers for quick meals.

### Choosing fish

1. There must be no unpleasant smell.
2. The flesh must be firm.
3. The tails must be stiff.
4. The gills must be red.
5. The eyes must be bright.
6. The scales on fish such as herrings must be plentiful.
7. The colouring on fish such as plaice and mackerel should be clear and bright.

### Storage of fish

Fresh fish is a highly perishable food and is best eaten on the day of purchase although it will keep till the following day in a refrigerator. To prevent the smell of fish pervading other foods in the refrigerator, it should be loosely covered and stored in the coolest part.

## Fish production and processing

Traditionally, fish has been gathered from the seas in large quantities and good quality white fish has been plentiful in the U.K. In recent years the quantity of white fish has been declining through over-fishing and we should be willing to use different varieties of fish. Fish farming is one way in which fish supplies can be increased, e.g. trout and salmon.

Fish is a highly perishable food which is often frozen for ease of transport and storage. It also needs care in the preparation and cooking, so food manufacturers sell some fish that has been filleted and coated ready to cook in a convenient frozen pack. This makes fish much more attractive to housewives and it was for this reason that fish fingers were developed, so that they could be cooked and served as quickly as sausages.

### *Methods of cooking fish*

*Preparation*: remove scales, entrails and fins of fish (and usually the head also). Wash well.

| HOW | WHY |
|---|---|
| *Boiling*: suitable for large fish. | |
| 1. Place fish into seasoned boiling water. | To retain the flavour, and to minimise the loss of soluble nutrients. |
| 2. Cover and simmer gently; allow 7–10 mins per 500 g and 10 mins over. | To avoid fish falling apart. |
| 3. Use the fish stock for making sauce. | To avoid waste of soluble nutrients. |
| *Steaming*: suitable for any fish, if not too large. | |
| Place in a steamer, or between two plates over a pan of boiling water. | Fish is cooked by direct or by indirect heat. |
| *Grilling*: suitable for small whole fish, or for steaks or fillets. | |
| 1. Slash whole fish along back. | To allow heat to penetrate. |
| 2. Brush cutlets or fillets with fat or oil. | To prevent them drying. |
| 3. Place under hot grill, turn fish during cooking and watch carefully. | To prevent burning. |

*Baking*: suitable for large fish or large cuts.

| | |
|---|---|
| 1. Prepare (this may include stuffing). | To improve flavour and food value. |
| 2. Put dabs of fat on fish. Cook in a moderate oven (160°C, Gas 3) allowing 7–10 mins per 500 g. | To prevent drying. |

*Frying*: suitable for small fish, steaks or fillets.

| | |
|---|---|
| 1. Fry oily fish without adding fat. Coat with oatmeal or flour. | Fat melts and runs out into pan from fish. |
| 2. Coat white fish with egg and breadcrumbs, or batter, and fry in shallow or deep fat. | To form a protective covering to fish and prevent drying. |

*Sousing*: suitable for herring and mackerel.

| | |
|---|---|
| 1. Place fish in casserole with vinegar, water, herbs and seasoning. Cover. | To add flavour and to keep fish moist. Acid softens bones so they are a good source of calcium. |
| 2. Bake gently in a slow oven until soft. | To prevent fish breaking up. |

## Eggs

Structure of eggs

1. A porous shell, mainly consisting of calcium carbonate.
2. Two shell membranes lying close together and lining the shell except at the large end of the egg, where they are separated and enclose the air space.
3. Egg white, consisting of a thick, sticky liquid (the albumen).
4. Egg yolk, surrounded by a thin membrane which extends into the white as 'balancers' holding the yolk in position (the chalazae).
5. The embryo, inside the yolk membrane.

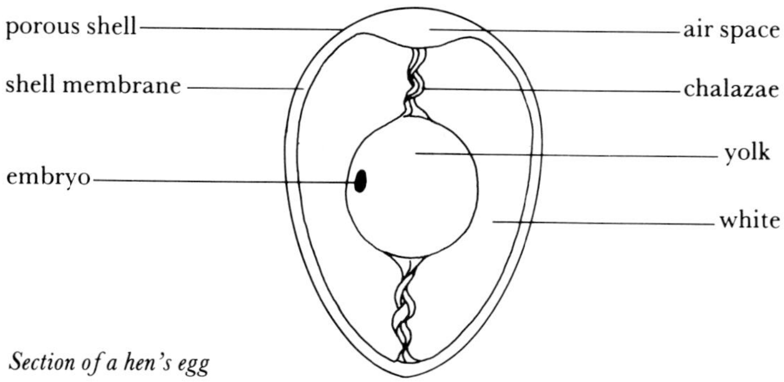


*Section of a hen's egg*

**Nutrient content**

The egg stores all the necessary nutrients for the growing chick. The approximate composition is:

| *Nutrient* | *Yolk* | *White* |
|---|---|---|
| Protein | 16% | 13% |
| Fat | 32% | Trace |
| Water | 51% | 86% |
| Minerals, vitamins, etc. | 1% | 1% |

In egg white the protein is albumin and in egg yolk it is vitellin; they are complete proteins of high biological value. The fat in the yolk is emulsified and easily digested. Yolk contains lecithin which is an emulsifier. The presence of the minerals calcium, phosphorus and iron, and the vitamins A, D, $B_1$ and $B_2$ in yolk make it more nutritious than egg white. An egg yolk weighs about 20 g and it contributes useful amounts of the above-named nutrients in an average diet.

Eggs contain no vitamin C or carbohydrate. As part of a balanced diet they should be served with foods supplying these nutrients, e.g. fruit or vegetables, bread or potatoes. Vitamin C aids the absorption of iron from egg yolk.

The energy value of an average egg is 380 kJ (90 kcal).

**Effect of cooking on eggs**

Egg white protein coagulates on heating at about 60°C, becoming white and firm.

Egg yolk proteins are mixed with fat and coagulate above 70°C, so the yolk remains softer than the white unless cooked for about 10 minutes.

The black discolouration around the yolk of hard-boiled eggs is caused by iron in the yolk reacting with hydrogen sulphide in the white. It can be avoided by cooling the eggs immediately after cooking.

If egg proteins are mixed with milk and heated, they combine with the liquid and cause thickening, e.g. baked egg custard forms a solid gel. If the custard is overcooked the proteins shrink and harden, causing 'curdling', and a watery fluid separates out.

**Digestibility of eggs**

Eggs are easily digested because, unlike meat or fish, they have no tough connective tissue. The fat is emulsified. They are therefore very suitable for invalids and young children. Egg white is most easily digested when lightly cooked.

**Use of eggs in cookery**

1. *As a main dish*: e.g. scrambled, fried, poached, boiled or in an omelette. Eggs supply animal protein of high biological value.
2. *Thickening*: e.g. in custards, sauces, soups and lemon curd. Egg proteins coagulate and combine with liquid on heating, causing thickening.
3. *Raising agent*: e.g. whisked egg sponges, hot soufflés. In flour mixtures, whisked egg holds air. The tiny bubbles of air expand on heating, thus causing the mixture to rise. The coagulation of

egg protein, when cooked, gives cakes a firm texture.
4. *Lightening*: e.g. cold soufflés and meringues. Air can be incorporated by whisked egg white.
5. *Binding*: e.g. stuffings and rissoles. The coagulation of proteins will hold dry ingredients together.
6. *Coating*: e.g. for fish or scotch eggs. Beaten egg, together with breadcrumbs, forms a protective covering for fried foods. The protein hardens and prevents the food absorbing too much fat, losing water and breaking up.
7. *Enriching*: eggs improve the nutritional value and the flavour of cakes, puddings and invalid drinks. The fat in egg yolk has a moistening and shortening effect in cakes.
8. *Emulsifying*: the oil and vinegar used to make mayonnaise would separate into two distinct layers if they were not emulsified with egg yolk. The egg yolk forms a film around each droplet of oil and keeps it suspended in the vinegar. The emulsifying action of the yolk makes the mixture thick and creamy.
9. *Glazing*: e.g. savoury pies and scones. Egg, or egg with milk, will give a shiny, brown colour to baked flour products. This is partly due to the Maillard browning reaction (see page 4).
10. *Garnishing*: egg adds colour to savoury dishes.

Quality of eggs

Eggs are sold by size, graded from the largest, size 1, to the smallest, size 7. The quality of eggs for retail is usually class A. To test for freshness:
1. The egg, held in front of a strong light, should show a small air pocket (the 'candling' test).
2. Place in a brine solution: 25 g salt in 250 ml water. A fresh egg will sink because it has a small air pocket. A less fresh egg will be suspended because the air pocket is larger, as the egg has dried out a little. A stale egg will float as it has a large air pocket. It may have dried out and gases may have been produced by the decaying egg.
3. On a plate, the yolk of a fresh egg will be domed and surrounded by thick white. In a stale egg, the yolk will be flattened and the white thin and spread out.

Storage and preservation of eggs

Store eggs in a cool place away from strong smelling foods as eggs readily absorb odours. They should always have the round end containing the air pocket uppermost as the yolk is then suspended centrally. Eggs do not need to be stored in a refrigerator where they tend to dry out if left too long. Fresh eggs should be bought each week.

Eggs can be preserved by closing the shell pores to prevent air and bacteria entering. This is done *either* by painting the shell with melted fat or wax, or with an egg varnish, e.g. Oteg; *or* by storing in a cold solution of sodium silicate (water glass).

Eggs may be frozen if they are first cracked and removed from the shell. Spare yolks or whites may be frozen for later use.

Duck eggs should not be preserved as they are sometimes contaminated with the food poisoning bacteria Salmonellae.

Egg production and packaging

Eggs are produced in vast numbers all the year round. There is very little difference in quality between fresh eggs from battery hens and those from free-range hens. Any noticeable difference is usually in the colour of the yolk.

Before packaging, eggs are checked for cracks or blemishes. They are 'candled' thus showing the size of the air space and any blood specks or cracked shells. They are weight-graded and packed in boxes. The boxes are labelled according to EEC regulations: numbers indicate the country of origin, the region of that country, and the packing station. The number of eggs, their size and quality classification, and the week number or date are also shown.

## Milk

Composition of milk

Milk is produced by female mammals for their young. Its composition varies with the type and condition of the animal and its diet. In humans, milk can supply the growing baby with most of the essential nutrients but as it lacks iron, vitamin C and dietary fibre, children of weaning age must be given meat, eggs and vegetables to supply these nutrients. Milk is too dilute to be the sole food for adults.

Nutrients in cow's milk (approximate percentages):

1. *Protein*: 3% animal protein, consisting of caseinogen, lactalbumin, and lactoglobulin.
2. *Carbohydrate*: 5% as lactose (milk sugar).
3. *Fat*: 4% animal or saturated fat, in the form of a fine emulsion.
4. *Minerals and vitamins*: 1% – chiefly calcium, phosphorus, sodium and potassium (there is very little iron); and vitamins A, D, $B_2$ (riboflavin). There are small amounts of vitamin $B_1$ (thiamin), nicotinic acid and vitamin C.
5. *Water*: 87%

The following table may help you learn the composition of milk:

| | |
|---|---|
| m | 1 |
| p | 3 |
| f | 4 |
| c | 5 |
| w | 87 |

## The nutrients in milk and how they behave

Proteins in milk

The chief protein in milk is caseinogen. It is combined with calcium and is only slightly soluble in water. In the stomach, the action of the enzyme rennin causes caseinogen to come out of solution and form curds of casein. Thus the commercial product Rennet, obtained from the rennin in calves' stomachs, when added to warm milk will cause the formation of casein curds and produce junket. Cheese is made from casein curds.

Milk is curdled by the action of acids such as lemon juice and lactic acid, which cause the caseinogen to come out of solution and clot.

The other proteins in milk are lactalbumin and lactoglobulin. These proteins are soluble and do not form curds, but they do coagulate on heating at about 60°C. They stick to the pan and form part of the skin. If heating continues, bubbles of steam form under the skin and make the milk boil over. These proteins are found in the whey of milk after cheese production.

The combination of amino acids in the three proteins is excellent for growth of mammals. It is of high biological value. Milk proteins are a good source of the essential amino acid lysine.

Fat in milk

The amount of fat in milk varies but in the UK different milks of varying fat content may be mixed to provide a minimum of 3% fat. Fat in whole milk is in fine droplets, or an emulsion, and is therefore easily digested. If milk is left to stand the droplets of fat join together, rise to the top and form a layer of cream. In homogenised milk the cream does not separate because the fat droplets have been made so small that they do not join together. Fat can be separated from whole milk to make cream or butter, leaving skimmed milk (which may be dried to a powder).

Fat in milk carries the fat soluble vitamins A (retinol) and D (calciferol).

Carbohydrate in milk

The milk sugar or lactose is not very sweet. It is easily digested by infants, not always by adults.

In sour milk the lactose is changed by bacteria (Lactobacilli) into lactic acid which then causes milk to clot, i.e. to separate into curds and whey. Lactic acid also causes the sour taste. This can be summarised:

$$\text{Lactose} \xrightarrow{\textit{Lactobacilli}} \text{lactic acid}$$

$$\text{Caseinogen} \xrightarrow{\textit{lactic acid}} \text{casein curds}$$

Minerals in milk

Milk is a good source of calcium and phosphorus. (It contains some vitamin D, calciferol, which is needed to absorb these minerals.) These substances are necessary for the formation of strong bones and teeth.

Milk contains very little iron, for this reason new born babies have a store of iron in their livers which lasts six months.

Vitamins in milk

Milk is a good source of vitamin A (retinol), especially when cows are eating green grass in the summer, the carotene in grass being converted to retinol in the cow.

Milk is the main source of vitamin $B_2$ (riboflavin) in the UK diet. Sunlight destroys this vitamin, so milk should not be left on the doorstep.

Vitamin D is created in the cow by the action of sunshine on fat in the skin and it is secreted in the milk.

**How milk is made safe to drink**

Milk is an ideal breeding ground for bacteria. At any time during its journey from cow to consumer it can become contaminated with harmful organisms, e.g. from a diseased cow, or from any person who handles it in transit, or from contaminated water or equipment. To make milk safe, the following precautions are taken:

1. Ensuring cows are healthy, e.g. tuberculin tested herds.
2. Ensuring no contamination arises from either the dairy workers or the equipment used.
3. Cooling the milk rapidly, after milking, to 7°C in order to discourage the growth of bacteria.
4. Treating the milk by heating to destroy bacteria, i.e. by pasteurisation or by sterilisation:

a) *Pasteurisation*: heat treatment which kills all *harmful* bacteria and most of the Lactobacilli (souring bacteria). In the high-temperature, short-time process (HTST), milk is heated to 72°C for fifteen seconds and then cooled to 10°C. Most milk sold in the UK is pasteurised; it is safe to consume, keeps well under refrigeration and is little changed in flavour or nutritive value.

b) *Sterilisation*: heat treatment which kills *all* bacteria. Sterilised milk may have a slightly 'cooked' flavour but it keeps well without refrigeration and is safe. There are two main methods of sterilisation: in the ultra-high temperature (UHT) method, a continuous flow of milk is heated to 150°C for one second and is then packed into sterile waxed cartons; in the second method, the already-bottled milk is heated at 100°C for half-an-hour.

**Importance of milk in the diet**

1. It is a particularly good source of protein, calcium, riboflavin and other B vitamins, and of vitamins A and D. Adolescents, pregnant and nursing mothers, and old people should all include milk in their diet as they have a particular need for these nutrients.
2. It is a natural and unrefined food with a good balance of most nutrients.
3. If pasteurised or sterilised, it is safe to drink and is easily available in the UK.
4. It is an inexpensive source of protein.
5. It is an easily digestible, nutritious food which is of great value to babies and invalids.
6. It has a bland flavour which enables it to be used in a variety of ways:

a) In beverages; plain or flavoured, e.g. milk shakes, cocoa.
b) With cereals, e.g. breakfast cereals, milk puddings or porridge.
c) In soups and sauces, both sweet and savoury.
d) In puddings, e.g. custards, junkets, milk jellies.
e) In flour mixtures, e.g. batters and cakes.

Types of milk

1. *Untreated*: available direct from the farm. The bottles have a green cap. It may also be in cartons.
2. *Pasteurised*: sold in cartons or in bottles with a silver cap.
3. *Channel island*: pasteurised milk from Jersey or Guernsey herds with a high fat content. It is sold in gold-capped bottles.
4. *Homogenised*: pasteurised milk with the fat evenly distributed so that there is no cream line. The bottles have a red cap.
5. *Ultra-heat treated milk (UHT)*: sometimes known as 'long-life' milk as it will keep, unopened, for several months without refrigeration. It is sold in cartons.
6. *Sterilised*: sold in bottles with a 'crown' cap, like beer.
7. *Canned milk*:

a) Evaporated: some of the water is removed, it is homogenised and sterilised. No sugar is added. Evaporation reduces the bulk and is convenient but the flavour is altered.
b) Condensed: very similar treatment but 40% sugar is added.

8. *Dried milk*: the powder may be either whole, full cream milk; skimmed milk, or filled milk made from skimmed milk with vegetable fats added. Instant milk powders have generally been prepared by a modified spray-drying process and they are quick and easy to reconstitute with water. They dissolve without forming lumps. Milk powder should not be used for feeding babies unless it is sold as special infant food when it will contain the correct proportions of minerals, vitamins and protein.

Storage of milk in the home

Keep milk cool, clean and covered in a dark place:
*Cool*: store in a refrigerator or in a cool place. In hot weather it can be covered with muslin hanging into a dish of cold water. As the water evaporates it cools the milk.
*Clean*: keep in bottles or cartons until required, or in clean milk jugs.
*Covered*: keep in bottles or cartons, or in jugs covered with muslin to exclude dust and flies. Covering will prevent milk absorbing flavours from other foods.
*Dark*: light breaks down riboflavin and ascorbic acid.

## Milk products

(Cream and butter do not contain proteins and are considered with other fats in Chapter 6.)

Yoghurt

Yoghurt is made from milk soured by specially grown yoghurt bacteria, e.g. Lactobacilli. Commercial yoghurt is usually made from skimmed milk and has a low fat content (1.5%). Yoghurt is a good source of protein, calcium and riboflavin; it may have added retinol and calciferol.

How to make yoghurt at home:

| HOW | WHY |
|---|---|
| 1. Place 2 teasp. fresh, natural yoghurt in a small container. | Natural yoghurt contains the special, live bacteria needed to 'culture' the milk. |
| 2. Add 1 teasp. sugar or honey. | For flavour. |
| 3. Stir in about 150 ml warm, sterilised (Longlife) milk. | Sterilised milk contains no live bacteria which would multiply and spoil the texture and flavour. |
| 4. Leave in a warm place for 7–8 hours until set. | Bacteria multiply in warm conditions. The lactose changes to lactic acid and this changes protein into soft, creamy curd. |
| 5. Store in a refrigerator until required. | Bacteria will stop making acid which would make the yoghurt too sharp and curdled. |

Yoghurt may be sweetened and flavoured with jam or stewed fruit. It may be served with breakfast cereals or added to casseroles, soups, sauces and salad dressings.

**Cheese**

Cheese and its composition

Cheese is an important milk product. Its composition varies according to the type of cheese and the milk from which it is made. Approximately 50 g of cheese can be made from 500 ml of milk and it contains most of the milk protein and fat. Cheese was originally a form of preserved milk made during summer when milk was plentiful.

The type of cheese made depends on:

a) The type of milk (from cow, goat or ewe).
b) The composition of the milk (whole or skimmed).
c) Whether acid or rennet is used for clotting.
d) The pressure applied during making.
e) The changes which occur during the ripening process due to enzymes, bacteria and moulds.

On average, hard cheese contains one-third protein, one-third fat and one-third water. The protein is of high biological value and supplements the protein in bread. The fat in cheese contains vitamin A. Cheese is an important source of calcium, phosphorus and vitamin $B_2$ (riboflavin).

Cheese contains no carbohydrate, iron or vitamin C but a well-balanced meal can be made by serving cheese with wholemeal bread and salad vegetables.

How cheese is made

1. *In the home, from soured milk*: e.g. cottage cheese. The lactic acid produced when unpasteurised milk sours, causes the coagulation of the milk proteins. The curd is then separated from the whey by being strained through muslin. The cheese is then seasoned and may also be flavoured with chives or parsley. Thus cottage

cheese may be made from cream, whole milk or skimmed milk.
2. *Commercially*: the milk is separated into curds and whey by the action of special cultures of bacteria, by heat and by rennet. The curd is separated from the whey, salted and pressed as dry as possible. It is then allowed to ripen in a cool place so that the characteristic flavour develops owing to the action of bacteria and moulds. Some commercial cheese is made from whole milk, some from skimmed milk and some from milk with added cream. The type of milk used determines the fat content of the finished cheese.
*Processed cheese*: this is made from Cheddar type cheese by grinding it to a pulp, or melting it with milk in steam-heated containers. This pasteurises the cheese and prevents the further action of enzymes and bacteria. It is mixed with emulsifiers and then cooled, moulded and packed.

Digestibility of cheese

In cooking, fat melts and the cheese softens. If heating is continued the protein hardens, shrinks and squeezes out the fat. In this state it is difficult to digest. Fat forms a waterproof layer around the cheese protein preventing the action of digestive enzymes in the stomach.
Digestibility can be improved by:
1. Chopping or grating finely.
2. Mixing with starchy foods such as potatoes or macaroni, or with flour in a cheese sauce (the starch will absorb some of the melted fat).
3. Serving with mustard or vinegar (these help stimulate the digestive juices).
4. Avoiding overcooking, as this causes the protein to shrink and harden. (Ensure other ingredients are cooked and hot before adding cheese, and do not keep hot too long.)

Uses of cheese in the diet

Cheese is a valuable source of protein, calcium and vitamins A and $B_2$. It is a way of preserving the food value of milk (which is perishable) in a concentrated form. It can be used in a variety of ways:
1. As a main dish to provide protein. Useful for vegetarians in macaroni cheese, cheese pie etc.
2. As a snack meal, e.g. Welsh rarebit, cheese and biscuits.
3. As a savoury course at the end of a meal, e.g. cheese straws.
4. As a flavouring in sauces, in pastry, in salads and sandwich fillings or as an accompaniment to risotto, soups and pasta dishes.
5. Curd cheese can be used in cheesecake.

Storage of cheese

1. In a refrigerator; either well wrapped or in a closed container, to prevent it from drying or from tainting other foods.
2. Wrapped in cling film or hung in a muslin bag and kept in a cool place.
3. Cheese may be stored in a freezer. It may become crumbly but can be used for grating and cooking.

# 4 Plant foods which provide protein

*Cereals and wheat products   Pulses   Nuts*

Some proteins are found in the mature seeds of plants, e.g. cereal grains, mature dried peas and beans (pulses), and nuts. When eaten as the only source of protein their usefulness for building our body proteins is limited. They are incomplete as one or more of the essential amino acids is missing, thus they are of low biological value. They are, however, of great value when combined with even small quantities of complete, or animal, proteins. They can be used as the only source of protein in a strict vegetarian diet provided a variety of them are eaten together. Starch is usually present in larger quantities than the protein in these plant foods.

## Cereals

These are the mature, edible seeds of cultivated grasses, e.g. wheat, maize, rice, oats, barley, rye. A great variety of foods is produced from these plants:
1. Wheat is made into flour for bread, cakes, pastries and biscuits; and into breakfast cereals, semolina and pasta, e.g. spaghetti and macaroni.
2. Maize is made into breakfast cereals, e.g. cornflakes, and into cornflour.
3. Rice is used as whole grain or as ground rice.
4. Oats are used for oatmeal and quick porridge oats.
5. Barley is used as a whole grain, or ground as patent barley.
6. Rye is used as a flour in some types of bread.

Importance of cereals in the diet

Cereals play an important part in our diet because:
1. Their growth is widespread and many parts of the world can produce one or more different cereal crops, therefore they are a readily available source of nutrients.
2. They are easily preserved when the seeds are ripe, and easily transported.
3. They are inexpensive compared with animal foods.
4. They are easy to prepare and digest.
5. They have no strong taste and can be made pleasant to eat in a variety of ways, both sweet and savoury.
6. They all contain starch; many also contain protein, B vitamins, mineral substances, fibre and fat.

*How cereals are used for our food*

Uses of cereals in the diet

1. As a staple item of diet, e.g. bread in Europe, rice in Asia, and maize in southern USA.

2. As a breakfast dish, e.g. porridge, or processed into prepared cereals. Flaked cereals are made by rolling the coarsely ground endosperm and then cooking it. Puffed cereals are prepared by heating the grains under pressure and then suddenly releasing the pressure so that the steam inside the grain expands rapidly, so puffing up the grain.
3. As the essential ingredient in cooking cakes, pastries and many puddings.
4. As the thickening agent in soups, sauces and gravies.

*Section of a cereal grain*

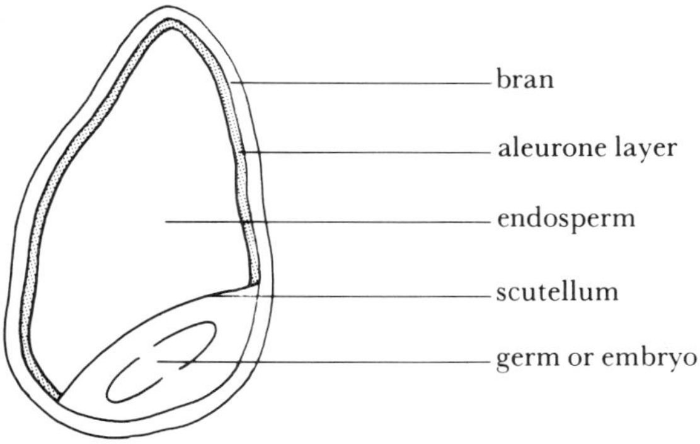


**Structure and composition of cereal grains**

Cereal grains all have a similar basic structure and composition:
*Bran*: 13%, on the outside of the grain, made of several thin layers containing cellulose, B vitamins and the mineral elements calcium and iron. The calcium and iron may be unavailable as they combine with phytic acid and form insoluble phytate salts.
*Endosperm*: 85%, consisting of thin walled cells (cellulose) containing starch grains separated by protein. The aleurone layer is the single-celled layer of endosperm nearest the bran and contains mostly protein with some B vitamins, minerals and phytic acid.
*Germ, or embryo*: 2%, is rich in proteins, fat, minerals and vitamins. The scutellum attaches the embryo to the endosperm and contains enzymes and vitamin $B_1$ (thiamin).

*The chief cereals used for food*

**Oats**

Oats supply much energy because they contain fat. They have a high protein content but no gluten (see page 45). Oats are ground to a fine, medium or coarse meal, or rolled to form flakes. They are used for porridge, oatcakes, for thickening soups and stews and for coating food for frying.

**Barley**

Barley is used for making malt in brewing. Barley in the household is used in small grains known as pearl barley, made by polishing the kernels after removing the husk. It may also be ground to a fine powder as patent barley. Either form may be used to prepare barley water, a cool and refreshing drink. Pearl barley is added to soups and stews.

**Maize**

When young and fresh, maize may be cooked as a vegetable and eaten as corn on the cob. When ripe, the endosperm may be ground to form cornflour, and used as the basis of custard powder, etc., or it may be coarsely ground and rolled to prepare breakfast cereals. Diets which depend on maize as the staple food tend to be deficient in nicotinic acid, one of the B vitamins, and this leads to the deficiency disease, pellagra.

**Rye**

Rye is grown in northern Europe. It has a distinctive flavour and can be used to make bread, as it will form gluten when mixed with water.

**Rice**

Rice is one of the least nutritious of cereals, containing the most starch and the least protein, fat and minerals. The bran and germ of unpolished rice contain protein, vitamin B, and minerals, but in polished rice these have been removed. The polished rice grains are sometimes parboiled and dried before polishing, this process causes a little of the vitamin B complex to be absorbed by the endosperm. From the time the rice is harvested, therefore, it is unfortunately subjected to a series of treatments – such as milling and polishing – which seriously deplete it of its nutrients. For example, 600 g unpolished, husked rice (2,200 kcal or 9.2 MJ) will provide 52 g protein, but a similar quantity of polished rice provides only 37 g. Where the diet consists of very little else this difference can be crucial. Bad storage, washing and cooking in excessive quantities of water will diminish the nutritive value of rice even more. Other important deficiencies in typical rice diets are in the B group vitamins, vitamin A and calcium.

Rice may be bought in the form of grains. Long grained, or Patna, rice may be brown (with the husk) or white. It is used chiefly for savoury dishes as the grains may be boiled in water and easily separated without forming a starchy mass. Short grained, or Carolina rice, is used chiefly for milk puddings where the free starch helps to thicken the milk. Rice can also be ground to a coarse powder and sold as ground rice for use in puddings, cakes and biscuits.

**Wheat**

The chief use of wheat in Britain is for the production of flour.

*How flour is made*:

1. The grains of wheat are cleaned.
2. They are put through rollers which split them, releasing the endosperm and breaking the outside layer of the grain into flakes.
3. This mixture, finely ground, produces wholemeal flour, i.e. a flour which contains all the nutrients of wheat.
4. If the germ and bran are removed after rolling and the remainder (chiefly endosperm) is ground, white flour is produced. If 100 parts of whole wheat are milled and sieved to produce 85 parts flour and 15 parts offals (bran+germ), the

flour is said to be 85% extraction. The average white flour in the UK is 73% extraction.

White flour of 73% extraction lacks the minerals and vitamins which are found in wholemeal flour. UK government legislation now requires the miller to add calcium, iron, thiamin and nicotinic acid to replace that lost in bran and germ. This is known as fortification.

Types of wheat flour

Wheat flour contains the proteins glutenin and gliadin. When mixed with water in a dough, the proteins form a sticky, elastic substance known as gluten. This gluten can trap bubbles of gas and hold the starch grains and fat globules. When heated, the elastic gluten is stretched by the expanding gases and later, being a protein, is 'set', or hardened, to form the framework of the cooked mixture. These properties of gluten form the basis of all types of bread, cake and pastry cooking.

Different varieties of wheat contain different amounts of protein, and the flours produced will have different uses:
*Strong flour*: is made from hard wheat grown in extreme climates, e.g. in Canada. It contains from 10–14% protein. The flour absorbs large amounts of liquid and makes a well-risen loaf of bread. It is the most suitable flour for all plain yeast mixtures, puff and flaky pastries and batters.
*Soft flour*: is made from soft, or weak, wheat grown in milder climates, e.g. in Britain. It produces flour with 8–10% protein. This flour is more suitable for cakes, biscuits and shortcrust pastry.
*Plain flour*: household flour blended from a mixture of strong and weak flours.
*Self-raising flour*: this has a raising agent already incorporated in it. The amount is usually that required to raise a plain cake mixture. It has the advantage of convenience, but the disadvantage that the amount of raising agent cannot be varied.
*Wholemeal flour*: this is 100% extraction. The bran and germ are included, possibly after heat treatment to reduce rancidity of the fat.
*Wheatmeal flour*: this is 80–92% extraction, having had the coarser particles of bran removed.
*High-ratio flour*: this is not widely available yet. It is very fine, soft, white flour which is used in cake mixtures with high proportions of sugar and liquid, e.g. in Angel cake and other light sponges. It produces a very tender cake crumb.

Nutritive value of wheat flour

Since the distribution of nutrients in the grain is not uniform, the content of the flour depends on its extraction rate or fortification. Wheat in the form of bread, flour, cakes, biscuits and pasta, provides more than one-quarter of the total energy, protein, carbohydrate and iron intake in the average UK diet. It also makes a substantial contribution to the intake of calcium, thiamin and nicotinic acid. Wheat flour contains between 8–14% proteins. These proteins are low in the essential amino acid lysine and so they are incomplete. Their usefulness for building our body proteins is limited by the lack of lysine. However, if flour or bread is eaten with even small quantities of milk, cheese, eggs, meat or fish, the missing lysine will be supplied and thus the value of the protein will be improved. The same effect is achieved by fortifying bread with dried milk powder or soya flour, or by serving baked beans on toast. These are more examples of the pairing or complementary effect of proteins. Where wheat and bread are staple items of diet, protein-energy malnutrition is rare.

Other wheat products supplying protein

*Bread*: bread and flour together supply 19% of the protein in an average UK diet. This is important, especially so where the intake of animal protein foods is low, e.g. in large families with low income. (See notes on bread in Chapter 5.)
*Semolina*: made from coarsely milled hard wheat and used for puddings and thickening soups.
*Pasta food*: e.g. macaroni, spaghetti and vermicelli, are made from strong flour which is first made into a paste with water. The high protein content enables the paste to be moulded into different shapes or into long threads or tubes. These are dried and partially cooked. They are used for dishes with meat or cheese or for milk puddings. The combination of proteins from pasta with milk, meat or cheese is an example of the 'pairing' of proteins.

**Pulses**

Pulses are the dried seeds of the Fabaceae family – peas, beans and lentils; they are sometimes called legumes. Their cultivation is widespread as they are capable of surviving in most climates and soils. They are an inexpensive source of protein and other nutrients. They are important in vegetarian diets and in countries where animal protein is unavailable or too expensive.

Nutritive value of pulses

Pulses are a good source of protein (20% dry weight). It is incomplete protein and methionine is the limiting amino acid. It is however a good source of lysine and so a combination of pulse and cereal proteins may have a nutritive value as high as animal proteins.

Pulses are a good source of the B vitamins thiamin and nicotinic acid.

Although pulses, like cereals, contain no ascorbic acid, it is produced during germination. So sprouted pulses are an excellent preventative against scurvy.

Pulses supply useful amounts of carbohydrate and iron.

Common varieties of pulses

The most widely eaten pulse in the UK diet is the canned 'baked bean', a type of haricot bean. Baked beans may be scorned by skilful cooks but they are a valuable food for some families: they are cheap, easily available, easy to store and prepare and, when eaten with bread, have a high nutritional value. This can be further improved by serving them with tomatoes and cheese.

Dried and processed peas are pulses. (Green peas as eaten in the UK are regarded as a fresh vegetable. They are usually immature seeds with a high water content and small amounts of carbohydrate and protein.)

Groundnuts or peanuts are not really nuts but pulses. When the seeds form, the flower stems turn down into the ground where the 'nuts' ripen. They are a rich source of protein and oil. Crushed peanuts can be used as a spread for bread. In countries where they form an important part of the diet they are often cooked in a kind of stew.

In other parts of the world various pulses (or dahl) are an important part of the diet, e.g. lentils, gram, cow pea, lima bean and locust bean.

Soya beans are pulses which are considered separately because of their importance.

Soya

Soya beans contain large amounts of protein and fat as well as starch. The beans have long been used in oriental cookery but only recently in the western world. Soya was cultivated in the USA as a source of edible oil for the manufacture of margarine, the protein by-product being used as animal food. More recently this high-protein soya meal has been processed for human use. The soya flour, containing both protein and starch, is added to sausages, biscuits, breakfast cereals and baby foods. Its function may not be primarily nutritional but it is added, in small amounts, to improve the texture of these processed foods.

*Processing of textured vegetable protein (TVP)*: the protein from soya beans can be processed to make a meat substitute known as textured vegetable protein, TVP. First the fat, starch and flavour ingredients are removed. The beans are crushed and the fat dissolved out. Then the starchy material may be washed out leaving the protein concentrate, or the protein may be isolated by dissolving it and filtering off the waste materials. The first type of process is less expensive than the second. The protein-rich material may then be coloured, flavoured and fortified with nutritional additives. It is then heated under pressure and extruded through a die, like a mincer plate. The material expands and acquires a texture similar to meat. Alternatively, the dissolved protein can be formed into a thread in a similar way to textile threads and then fabricated into a meat-like material, e.g. Kesp.

*Uses of TVP*: it may be used in two ways: a) As a *meat extender* if it is intended to replace only *part* of the meat in a dish. The TVP is generally in a dry form and can be reconstituted by boiling in stock. It is cheaper than meat and so provides a good way of economising. b) As a *meat substitute*, TVP can be used in dishes to replace meat. It is best used in dishes with a distinctive flavour like curry. It is a good source of protein for vegetarians.

TVP has several advantages apart from low cost. In dry form it is light weight, it can be stored easily, there is no waste fat or gristle, it is quick to prepare. The disadvantage of poor flavour and texture may be overcome by applied technology but at the moment this is too costly to be worthwhile.

*Nutritional value of TVP*: it should be compared with meat as it replaces meat in the diet. Although in the UK there are no regulations at present, it has been suggested that novel protein foods such as TVP should contain 50% protein with the essential amino acid methionine added; plus iron, thiamin, riboflavin and vitamin $B_{12}$. Where necessary, these may be added by the manufacturer.

**Nuts**

Value of nuts in the diet

Nuts, among which we include almonds, walnuts, cashews, brazils, hazels, cobs, pecans and pistachios, form another valuable food. Their protein content is similar to that of dried peas and beans but, as they are not soaked before cooking, weight for weight they are a richer source of vegetable protein. They also contain fat, carbohydrate, some mineral salts and vitamins of the B complex.

Nuts contain a large amount of roughage and are therefore difficult to digest unless they are chewed well. They may be minced or ground before being used. They are used largely in vegetarian dishes, in stuffings, in cakes and sweets, or served as a dessert.

# 5 Foods which provide carbohydrates

*Starchy foods not already covered (bread, potatoes, sugars)   Fruits*
*Vegetables   Salads*

As mentioned in the earlier section on carbohydrates, there are three important groups: starches, sugars and dietary fibre or unavailable carbohydrates.

Sources of starch

1. *Cereals*: these foods are important sources of both starch and protein in most diets. They form staple items of diet all over the world. (See Chapter 4 for wheat and wheat products, rice, maize, oats, barley.)
2. *Potatoes*: a staple vegetable widely grown in Europe and America.
3. *Sago*: made from the pith of the sago palm.
4. *Tapioca*: made from the roots of the cassava plant.
5. *Arrowroot*: made from the underground stem of the maranta.

The last three are not staple foods in the West; they are used mainly for milk puddings or for thickening soups and sauces.

**Bread**

Types of bread

*White bread* made from 73% extraction flour, fortified during milling.
*Wholemeal bread* made from 100% extraction flour.
*Wheatmeal bread* made from 80–92% extraction flour.
(Both these types of bread are valued for their flavour, texture and fibre content.)
*Speciality loaves*: milk and soya-enriched bread have protein of high biological value. Germ breads are enriched with extra vitamins and minerals from added germ. Starch-reduced breads have added gluten and the term should only be applied to bread with less than 50% carbohydrate.

Value of bread in the diet

1. It is reasonably cheap.
2. It has no strong flavour and can be eaten with a wide variety of other foods.
3. It is easily digested; white bread probably more easily than wholemeal bread owing to the absence of fibre.
4. It is one of the main sources of energy in the average UK diet. It contains 50% carbohydrate and 8% protein. It is an important source of protein as relatively large amounts of bread are eaten daily.

5. Iron, calcium, thiamin and nicotinic acid are present in wholemeal flour. They are added to white flour by the miller. Some iron and calcium in wholemeal bread may be unavailable owing to the presence of phytic acid with which they form insoluble salts.
6. Wholemeal bread can be a valuable source of dietary fibre.

**Potatoes**
The potato is so widely available in Europe that its importance may be overlooked. Potatoes are easily grown and yield more energy per acre than any cereal. Their nutrient content is such that, when eaten alone in sufficient quantity, they will support life, e.g. in Ireland before the potato famine of the nineteenth century.

Potatoes are a nutritious, whole food. They contain 17–20% starch, 2% protein and useful amounts of ascorbic acid, thiamin and iron. The protein has good biological value. New potatoes have a higher ascorbic acid content than old ones that have been stored. Potatoes are a valuable food for low income families, especially when supplemented by margarine, milk or cheese, and green vegetables.

**Sugars**
Sugar (sucrose) is produced from sugar cane and from sugar beet. It is present in all ripe and dried fruits.

Production of sugar

1. The beets or canes are crushed and the sugar extracted with water.
2. This is purified by adding lime, and bubbling carbon dioxide through the solution.
3. It is then concentrated by evaporation and crystals of brown sugar form. These are separated from the remaining brown liquid which is called molasses or treacle.
4. The crystals are re-dissolved and purified.
5. The liquid is again evaporated and crystals of white sugar are formed. The liquid left is golden syrup.

Types of sugar

1. *Lump, or loaf sugar*: compressed and cut into even-sized lumps.
2. *Granulated sugar*: consists of coarse crystals suitable for sweetening dishes in cooking.
3. *Caster sugar*: consists of finer crystals and is suitable for cakemaking because it dissolves readily; also for sprinkling over sweet dishes.
4. *Icing sugar*: very finely ground sugar used for all icing mixtures and for sprinkling over cakes.
5. *Demerara sugar*: consists of coarse crystals mixed with molasses. This gives it a distinctive flavour and colour but little extra nutritional value.
6. *Moist brown sugar*: this has smaller crystals, is dark in colour and contains more moisture and molasses.

7. *Raw molasses*: contains small amounts of calcium, iron and B vitamin.

Treacle and syrup are by-products in the refining of sugar. They contain some invert sugar (glucose and fructose) which inhibits crystallisation of the sucrose. Dark treacle does contain useful amounts of iron. Both treacle and syrup are used in cake and pudding making, and as spreads for bread.

Honey contains about 75% invert sugar as well as some sucrose. Jams supply us with sucrose (added during the cooking for preservation) and some invert sugar formed during boiling.

Glucose is a simple sugar made commercially from starch. It is a mild sweetening agent. It is used as a quick energy food as it requires no digestion and is rapidly absorbed into the bloodstream.

Value of sugars in the diet

Sugars, syrups, honey and jams should not be considered as sources of nutrients. They provide energy but do not contain the B vitamins which are necessary for the efficient release of this energy. They are palatable, cheap and readily available. For these reasons, over-consumption is a danger. These foods tend to displace more nutritious foods, e.g. bread and potatoes, from the diet of people most at risk, i.e. the poor and the ignorant. The high sugar consumption in western society is associated with an increase in tooth decay, obesity, diabetes and heart disease.

**Fruits**

Fruits are seed-bearing parts of plants; during ripening they become fleshy, succulent and sweet.

Importance of fruit in the diet

1. When fruits are formed, food reserves are laid down as starches and pectin. As the fruits ripen, the starch is changed to sugars.
2. They contain mineral substances, chiefly potassium, phosphorus, calcium, manganese and a little iron.
3. They supply indigestible dietary fibre, especially the cellulose in the skins and seeds.
4. All fruits supply water, some, like melon, as much as 94%.
5. Fruits supply varying amounts of ascorbic acid (vitamin C). Some fruits such as blackcurrants, strawberries and citrus fruits are particularly rich sources. In addition, all orange-coloured fruits such as oranges, apricots and peaches supply carotene which the body can change into retinol (vitamin A).
6. Fruits also contain organic acids which form the salts which give them their individual flavour.
7. Fruits are palatable and refreshing adding variety to the diet in many ways.

Uses of fruit in the diet

1. As a raw dessert. Crisp fruit is useful for cleaning the teeth.
2. As preserves in jam, jelly, marmalade and chutney.
3. As cooked fruit either stewed, baked or fried.

4. Combined with flour mixtures, e.g. pastry, batters.
5. In cold sweets, e.g. fruit foods, salads, mousses, jellies.
6. Dried fruits, e.g. sultanas, raisins, currants, give variety to cakes and puddings.
7. As drinks: fruit juices, squash and cordials; in wines and liqueurs.

Effects of cooking on fruit

1. The pectin, which joins the cell walls to make tissues, dissolves in warm acid conditions and the tissues are softened.
2. The cellulose cell walls are softened.
3. Owing to the acidity of fruit there is only a little destruction of ascorbic acid.
4. Soluble nutrients pass into the cooking liquid, but as this is usually served with the fruit there is no loss.
5. Enzymes, for example those which cause browning of pale fruit like apples, are inactivated by boiling.

## Vegetables

Vegetables are usually classified according to the part of the plant from which they come:
a) Roots, e.g. carrots, turnips.
b) Bulbs, e.g. onions, shallots.
c) Tubers, e.g. potatoes, Jerusalem artichokes, yams.
d) Stems, e.g. celery, leeks.
e) Leaves, e.g. cabbage, sprouts.
f) Flowers, e.g. cauliflower, flowering broccoli.
g) Fruits, e.g. tomatoes, cucumbers, marrows.
h) Seeds, e.g. peas, broad beans.

Importance of vegetables in the diet

1. They provide vitamins: Carotene in red, yellow and green vegetables can be turned by the body into retinol (vitamin A) and stored in the liver. Some of the B vitamins are present in potatoes, green vegetables and pulses. Ascorbic acid (vitamin C) is present in all green vegetables, in potatoes and in some salad vegetables.

Care is necessary in preparation and cooking to preserve this vitamin.
2. They provide mineral elements such as potassium, phosphorus, calcium, magnesium, iron and in some cases iodine.
3. The large amount of cellulose is useful to the body as indigestible fibre.
4. When young, vegetables such as onions, carrots and peas contain sugar; and potatoes and dry peas and beans contain starch. These carbohydrates supply energy.
5. Some vegetables such as the pulses, peas, beans and lentils supply useful amounts of protein. Green leafy vegetables do not contain protein.
6. All vegetables supply water, most contain from 70–95%.
7. They supply variety in colour, flavour and texture in the diet.

Uses of vegetables in the diet

1. As an accompaniment to the main foods, e.g. potatoes, root and green vegetables and salads with meat.
2. As the main part of a vegetarian meal. A variety of vegetables including peas, beans and lentils are served, sometimes accompanied by pastry and eggs, milk or cheese for the complementation of proteins.
3. As the main ingredient in soups, or as purées for infants and invalids, e.g. celery, carrots.
4. As preserves in pickles and chutneys, e.g. cucumber, onion.
5. As ingredients in sauces, e.g. tomato, onion, mushroom.
6. As garnishes, e.g. tomato, watercress.

Cooking vegetables

Ascorbic acid is easily lost from vegetables during cooking both through oxidisation and through being dissolved in water. Oxidisation can occur by free access to air and is accelerated by the enzyme oxidase from cut and damaged cells, by warmth, by alkali and by traces of copper.

The aims in cooking vegetables are:

1. To preserve all the nutrients, especially the minerals and vitamins B and C.
2. To make them more palatable and digestible. During cooking, the cellulose framework is softened, starch grains absorb water and are gelatinised.
3. To use them as fresh as possible. Home-grown vegetables have the best food value, flavour and texture.

*Preparation of vegetables for cooking*

They must be trimmed and washed thoroughly to remove dirt and insects but they should not be soaked as ascorbic acid is soluble in water. New potatoes should be scraped or peeled thinly just before cooking. Do not soak them in water. If exposed to the air, enzymes cause peeled potatoes to discolour.

Root vegetables and onions, remove the outside skin thinly. Pulses are easier to cook if soaked in boiled (soft) water for 12–24 hours.

Frozen vegetables require no preparation and should not be thawed prior to cooking.

Leaf vegetables must be shredded just before cooking. Cut cells release the enzyme oxidase which destroys ascorbic acid.

*Choice of method*

Choose a method suitable for the type of vegetable, using a conservative method where possible (i.e. one which conserves the nutrients). Thus, cook potatoes in their skins, cook green vegetables and roots as quickly as possible in the minimum of water.

Pressure cooking and steaming are suitable for roots and potatoes. There is no loss of soluble nutrients as the vegetable does not touch the water. Steaming is not suitable for green vegetables, the long cooking necessary spoils the colour and destroys the vitamin C. Stewing or braising is suitable for roots and onions. All soluble nutrients are retained. Carrots etc. may be cooked in an oven casserole. Frying, baking and roasting are suitable for potatoes and some roots. Grilling is suitable for vegetables which soften easily, e.g. tomatoes and mushrooms. Sautéing, or fat-steaming, is suitable for sliced leeks and courgettes.

*The conservative method of boiling green and root vegetables:*

| HOW | WHY |
|---|---|
| 1. Prepare and cut the vegetables into small pieces, shred cabbage. | For quick cooking. |
| 2. Put about 2 cm depth of water in a pan. Bring to the boil. | Little water means less loss of soluble nutrients. Boiling water inactivates the enzyme oxidase. |
| 3. Place vegetables in pan. Add salt (1 teasp./500 ml water). | To improve flavour. |
| 4. Cover with fitting lid and bring back to boil. Boil for about 10 minutes. Boil gently. | To prevent evaporation. To cook until just tender. To prevent the vegetables breaking into small pieces. |
| 5. Strain off liquid, to be used for soup or gravy. | To save nutrients which have dissolved in the water. |
| 6. Serve vegetables at once. | If kept warm, the vitamins are easily lost. |

## Salads

A salad is a mixture of vegetables or fruits, or sometimes both. The ingredients may be cooked but are more often served raw. Salads are not usually a good source of energy but this may be supplied by oil in a good salad dressing. Protein is often added in the form of meat, eggs, cheese or nuts. Strong flavours must be used sparingly, e.g. onions, garlic, chives.

Value of salads in the diet

1. To supply vitamins: chiefly carotene and ascorbic acid as found in green vegetables, peppers and tomatoes.
2. To supply mineral elements: chiefly calcium, potassium, iron and phosphorus.
3. To supply dietary fibre. If served raw, vegetables must be young and tender, or finely grated, or chopped.
4. To give variety to meals in colour, texture and flavour.

*Making salads*

| **HOW** | **WHY** |
|---|---|
| 1. Ensure all ingredients are fresh. | They then have maximum food value. |
| 2. Wash but do not soak. | To clean but to avoid loss of soluble nutrients. |
| 3. Serve immediately they are prepared. | To avoid loss of vitamins. |
| 4. Avoid shredding too finely unless vegetables are coarse. | Enzymes are set free that destroy the vitamins. |
| 5. Arrange attractively. A flat dish gives the best display. | To encourage appetite. |
| 6. Serve with a suitable dressing. | To supply additional food nutrients and to enhance flavour. |

Types of salad

*Savoury salads:*
1. Green salad using lettuce, watercress, sliced cucumber and green pepper, spring onions.
2. Mixed salad using lettuce, cress, sliced cucumber, tomatoes, radishes, grated carrots.
3. Cooked vegetable salads, e.g. potato salad, Russian salad and bean salads with a dressing.
4. Mixtures of fruits and vegetables, e.g. orange, lettuce and watercress.

*Sweet salads:*
Fruit salads may contain any fruit in season, or tinned or bottled fruit. The fruit may be raw or cooked, but must be cut into neat even-sized pieces. It is served in a syrup of sugar, lemon juice and water, often accompanied by cream, ice-cream, junket or custard. The success of a fruit salad depends upon the skilful blending of colour and flavour.

Salad dressings

1. A French dressing of seasoned oil with vinegar or lemon juice is served with green salads. The dressing may be served separately and the green leaves tossed in the dressing at the table just before serving.
2. A mayonnaise made of oil and vinegar emulsified with egg yolks may be served with any vegetable salad. It is particularly good with eggs, cold fish or chicken salads.
3. A cooked salad dressing is often made by flavouring a thin white sauce. This may be used with any type of vegetable salad, e.g. coleslaw.

# 6 Foods which provide fats

*Animal and vegetable fats   Their food value   Use of fats*

Fats and oils are found both in animals and plants. Animals make them from fats and carbohydrates in their food; plants make them from starches and sugars.

We get animal fats from meat, milk and milk products. We get vegetable fats and oils from fruits and seeds, e.g. olives, nuts. Some fish contain oils in their flesh, e.g. mackerel, salmon.

Value of fats in the diet

1. To supply the body with fat which is a concentrated source of energy, and fat-soluble vitamins.
2. To enable us to add variety by frying and roasting foods.
3. To make dry foods, such as bread, more palatable and easy to eat.
4. To improve the texture of flour doughs, i.e. as shorteners in pastry and cakes.

**Common fats**

Cream

Cream consists of the fat from milk plus varying amounts of water. It does not contain useful amounts of any nutrient other than fat and vitamin A. It is a luxury product with a smooth texture. The amount of fat varies:
1. *Half cream*: 12% fat, will not whip.
2. *Single cream*: 18% fat, will not whip.
3. *Whipping cream*: 35% fat. This is the minimum amount of fat necessary for whipping.
4. *Double cream*: 48% fat (minimum). It may be homogenised to make it thicker.
5. *Clotted cream*: 55% fat, usually from Devonshire or Cornwall. It is made by skimming the fat from pans of scalded milk.
6. *Sterilised cream*: 23% fat, will not whip. It will keep for two years, unopened.
7. *Ultra-heat treated (UHT) cream*: variable fat content. Available in cartons. Will keep if unopened.
8. *Imitation cream*: variable fat content. Made from refined vegetable oils and skimmed milk solids.

Home-made cream can be made economically by melting 100 g unsalted butter with half-a-teaspoon gelatine in 100 ml warm milk (38°C), and mixing in a liquidiser at top speed for one-and-a-half minutes. It is then allowed to stand in a covered bowl in a refrigerator overnight and can be used in the same way as double cream.

**Butter**

Cream is pasteurised and then allowed to ripen by the action of bacteria. These cause it to develop certain characteristic flavours, and a degree of acidity which breaks up the emulsion; the fat globules then cling together. The mixture is churned to separate the liquid or buttermilk. Salt is added and the butter 'worked' until it is smooth in texture. Butter contains up to 16% water and variable amounts of vitamins A and D. It is a refined source of saturated fat (see Chapter 1).

**Margarine**

Oils from groundnuts, soya beans, palm fruit and palm kernel, coconuts and whale oil are purified and hardened by the addition of hydrogen so that they make a solid fat (see page 7). The unsaturated fatty acids take up the hydrogen and are converted to saturated fatty acids. The solid fat is mixed with milk, salt, flavour, colour and vitamins A and D. The mixture is then churned to make it the consistency of butter.

Butter and hard margarine are used for similar cookery processes. They are both suitable for cakes, pastries and biscuits but butter has a slightly better flavour. Margarine and butter are only suitable for low temperature, shallow frying.

Special margarines can be made with different properties. Soft margarines are made which are spreadable at low temperatures. They often have emulsifiers added which assists creaming in cake making. Some soft margarines are made with a high content of polyunsaturated fats. They have approximately the same energy value as other margarines but they may be used to replace saturated fats where a person is at risk from coronary heart disease.

Low fat spreads, e.g. Outline, cannot be called margarines because they have a much lower fat content. They contain more water and so have a lower energy value, hence their value in a slimming diet.

**Shortening (white cooking fats)**

These are made from hardened oils in the same way as margarine. The fats may have air incorporated to give a creamy texture. They may be used for pastry making or frying.

**Animal cooking fats**

*Lard* is 100% fat and is obtained from the pig. It is good for frying. It does not cream well with sugar. It rubs easily into flour and gives good short texture in pastry.

*Suet* is a hard fat obtained from mutton or beef. It is usually taken from around the kidneys. It is too hard to rub into flour so it is chopped or grated and used for suet pastry, puddings or stuffings.

*Dripping* is the melted fat obtained from cooked carcass meat. Its flavour varies with the animal from which it is obtained.

**Oils**

Edible oils are liquid fats usually containing many polyunsaturated fatty acids. They have a similar energy value to hard fats but they have a lower melting point (at normal room temperature they are in the liquid state). They may be used for frying, salad dressings and for cake and pastry making. The chief cooking oils are obtained from maize, groundnuts, soya beans and palm kernels. Olive oil has a distinctive flavour for salad dressings. Oils obtained from the liver of white fish are rich sources of vitamins A and D.

**Rendering fat**

This is to extract fat from animal tissues to use as dripping. When meat is bought in bulk for the freezer, the fatty trimmings should be cut into small pieces and placed in a tin in a slow oven until the fat has melted. The fat may then be poured off and allowed to cool and harden. Dripping may be used for frying and it can be stored in the freezer for up to 6 months.

**Clarifying fat**

Place the fat in a pan and cover it with water. Heat gently until the water is boiling. Pour into a basin. When cool, remove the solid fat from the top and scrape the bottom to remove impurities. Gently heat the fat again until all bubbling stops: the residual water will have then evaporated. Cool.

**Storage of fats and oils**

Fats may be turned rancid by the action of bacteria which break up the fat into fatty acids and glycerol. This may be prevented by storing solid fat at a low temperature, wrapped in greaseproof paper. Oils should be stored in stoppered bottles at room temperature. If kept very cold they will, of course, solidify.

**Use of fats**

1. For frying (see page 79).
2. For shortening in pastries (see page 89) and cakes (page 95).
3. For the inclusion of air, e.g. the creaming method of cake making, and in whipped cream.
4. To increase the energy value of some dishes, e.g. salad dressings.
5. To provide a smooth, creamy texture, e.g. cream in mousse and ice-cream.
6. To develop flavour, e.g. fat-steaming (sautéing) vegetables in soup making.
7. To retain succulence, e.g. basting of meat.
8. To prevent sticking on baking pans. (Use lard or white fat for this purpose.)

# 7 Meal planning

*General principles Meal planning Shopping and budgeting*
*Planning for special groups Meals for special occasions*
*Economy in catering Left-over food Time planning*

## General principles of meal planning

The balanced diet

A good diet is one which provides all the nutrients in the correct proportions to suit the individual. A well-balanced meal not only provides this diet but the choice of foods served is attractive, and varied in colour, texture, flavour and appearance.
To maintain good health the balanced diet must contain:
1. Animal and plant foods containing protein; sometimes called main foods.
2. Foods containing carbohydrates and fats; sometimes called fillers.
3. Fruits and vegetables.
4. Watery drinks.

In practical terms the following foods should be included in the daily diet of the normal healthy adult:

| HOW | WHY |
|---|---|
| 500 ml milk. | To supply animal protein, fat, milk sugar, vitamins A, $B_2$, D, calcium and phosphorus. |
| 50–100 g cooked meat or fish; liver occasionally. | To supply animal proteins, fat, B complex vitamins, iron. |
| 1 egg. (No more than 4 a week.) | To supply protein, fat, vitamins, iron. |
| 50 g cheese, nuts, pulses or additional meat. | To supply additional protein, vitamins, etc. |
| 200 g bread, preferably wholemeal. | To supply carbohydrate, protein, iron, calcium and vitamins $B_1$ and nicotinic acid. |
| 1 serving of potato.<br>1 serving of green or yellow vegetable.<br>1 serving of another vegetable, preferably uncooked.<br>1 serving of fruit. | To supply carbohydrate, dietary fibre, minerals, vitamins A and C. |

| | |
|---|---|
| 50 g butter or margarine. | To supply fat, vitamins A and D. |

About $1\frac{1}{2}$ litres water in tea, coffee or other beverage.

Provision of nutrients in the balanced diet

The nutrients listed below will be adequately supplied if the diet includes some of the foods mentioned in each case:
1. *Protein*: include meat, eggs, cheese, fish, milk, pulses or TVP, and nuts.
2. *Fat*: include butter, margarine or oils.
3. *Carbohydrate*: include bread, potatoes and some cakes, pastries, preserves or sugar.
4. *Vitamins*:
A: include milk, cheese, butter, margarine, green, yellow or red vegetables.
$B_1$ and nicotinic acid: include bread, meat, yeast.
$B_2$: include milk, cheese and eggs.
C: include fresh fruit and vegetables, orange juice for infants.
D: include margarine, milk and butter.
5. *Minerals*:
For iron: include meat, liver, bread, watercress.
For calcium: include milk, cheese, bread.
For iodine: include fish, iodised salt.
For sodium: include salt.
For other minerals: include natural, unrefined foods, fruit and vegetables.
6. *Dietary fibre*: include wholemeal cereals or bran, vegetables and fruit.
7. *Water*: include plenty of drinks, soups, sauces and fruit.

**Meal planning**

The following points must all be considered when planning meals:

Important factors in meal planning

1. The nutritional value of the foods so that a balanced diet is provided.
2. The nutritional requirements of individuals: this will be related to their age, sex, type of work and state of health. The requirements of special groups will be considered later (page 62).
3. The occasion for which the meal is required, e.g. party or family.
4. The provision of an attractive variety of colours, flavours, and textures:
a) Do not serve all foods of a similar colour, e.g. fish, cauliflower and creamed potato.
b) Use carrots, tomatoes and green vegetables to give variety of colour.

c) Use garnishes for colour.
d) Do not serve similar foods in the same meal, e.g. beef soup followed by beef-steak pie, or a grapefruit starter followed by a fruit salad dessert.
e) Contrast the textures of the foods: some soft and some crisp, some hot and some cold, some cooked and some raw.
f) Avoid serving pastry dishes in successive courses, or stewed meat and stewed fruit in the same meal.
5. The season of the year. Serve foods which suit the external conditions, e.g. hot pies and puddings in cold weather, salads in warmer weather. Use foods which are of good quality. Use home-grown produce.
6. The money available and the number of people to be catered for: it is important to be able to work within whatever budget is set, whether it is for an economical meal or a party meal.
7. Time available for preparation and cooking. This is important if the cook is away from home most of the day. In this case convenience foods are helpful and should be chosen from frozen, canned or dry goods which are already prepared. Planning ahead is necessary so that one bulk mixture may be used for two meals, e.g. a casserole, or a pastry or cake mix.
8. The time of the meal: an inexperienced cook must plan ahead so that all dishes can be served at the correct time. The meal plan must suit the time of day and the needs of the individuals. The main meal is served when the family are all at home. This may be either midday or evening.
9. The cooking facilities and capabilities of the cook: number of pans, size of tins, type of cooker, fuel economy, use of automatic timing. Do not attempt all hot or elaborate dishes if inexperienced.
10. Shopping and storage facilities: use of food from larder, refrigerator and freezer; availability in local shops.

## How to budget and shop

The following points must be considered carefully:

1. Decide how much of the family income can be spent on food.
2. Study the standard prices of the main foods.
3. Plan meals for several days together, for economy of cost and time.
4. Prepare a shopping list, which may be adapted to take advantage of genuine bargains.
5. Shop where the shopkeeper pays attention to the hygiene of premises and assistants.
6. Whenever possible buy in large quantities. Adequate storage for dry goods and root vegetables helps here, as does possession of a refrigerator and/or a freezer.
7. Buy green vegetables and fruit as fresh as possible.

**Points for economy when shopping**

1. Select cheaper protein foods, e.g. cheese, milk, pulses, rather than meat.
2. Select cheaper cuts of fish and meat, e.g. stewing meat rather than roasting joints.
3. Use sprouts or cabbage as sources of vitamin C rather than fresh fruit. Locally grown vegetables are often cheaper than imported fruit.
4. Use a cooking method which is economical of fuel, e.g. cooking a whole meal at once in the oven, or in one steamer.
5. Avoid buying too much and use up all left-over foods.

## Planning meals for special groups

**Vegetarian meals**

| HOW | WHY |
|---|---|
| 1. Find out whether the food is for (a) Strict vegetarians (vegans) | They eat nothing of animal origin; usually either for reasons of health or religion (though many will drink milk). |
| *or* (b) Lacto-vegetarians. | They do not eat anything killed for food, e.g. meat, fish, or poultry, but they do eat eggs, cheese and milk dishes. |
| 2. Include adequate protein to replace meat, etc. for body-building. | For strict vegetarians, use TVP, pulses, nuts and wholemeal cereals. For lacto-vegetarians use dairy foods as well. |
| 3. Season and flavour food well, using herbs, spices, etc. | To overcome the blandness of some vegetable foods. |
| 4. Use vegetable fats or oils for cooking. | To avoid the use of animal fats such as lard and dripping. |
| 5. Use vegetable extracts, e.g. Marmite, for flavouring gravies, etc. | To avoid the use of animal extracts. |
| 6. Avoid too much carbohydrate. | Vegetarian diet tends to contain too much carbohydrate food and be too bulky. |
| 7. Introduce variety and colour in the vegetables and serve them attractively. Use tomatoes, onions, celery and mushrooms. | They have a good savoury flavour. |
| 8. Serve some raw foods, e.g. fruits and salads. | To supply minerals and vitamins. |

| | |
|---|---|
| 9. Use wholemeal cereals and wholemeal flour. | To supply more protein and minerals. |
| 10. If digestion is poor, give vegetables sieved as purées or as soups. | To avoid too much dietary fibre. |

Vegetarian dishes

*Soups*: lentil, pea or vegetable purées, enriched with milk for lacto-vegetarians.
*Main meal dishes*: vegetable pie, pasty or flan. Vegetable stew, risotto or curried vegetables. Nut cutlets or TVP substitute meat.
Lacto-vegetarians can also eat macaroni cheese, vegetables with cheese sauce, cheese pudding or soufflé, curried or stuffed eggs, omelettes.
Any of these dishes may be served with a selection of salads or cooked vegetables.
*Breakfast dishes*: fresh fruit, cereals, porridge or muesli. Toast with marmalade, peanut butter or marmite. For lacto-vegetarians, any egg dish such as an omelette, boiled or scrambled egg.
*Snacks and supper dishes*: vegetable tarts or pasties, salad sandwiches, mushrooms on toast, green salads with nuts. Lacto-vegetarians will also eat egg or cheese salads, cheese flan or straws.
*Sweets or puddings*: any fruit, fresh or cooked. Fruit, jam or nut pastries, avoiding the use of animal fats. Lacto-vegetarians may be served with desserts made from milk, gelatine or eggs.

*A typical day's menu for a lacto-vegetarian:*
*Breakfast*: grapefruit, scrambled egg on toast, wholemeal bread and butter, marmalade or honey, tea or coffee.
*Dinner*: lentil soup, cheese and tomato flan, a green vegetable. Stewed fruit and custard.
*Tea*: wholemeal scones and butter, fresh fruit and tea.
*Supper*: salad with nuts or cheese, baked jacket potatoes. Baked egg custard and fruit. A milk or fruit drink before bedtime.

*A typical day's menu for a strict vegetarian:*
*Breakfast*: fresh orange juice, stewed prunes with cereal, toasted wholemeal bread with margarine and marmalade or peanut butter. Black coffee or cocoa, or lemon tea.
*Dinner*: lentil soup, or TVP in curry with rice and side dishes, or rice and corn salad with mixed raw vegetables (including watercress, chopped cabbage, shredded carrots, tomatoes and lettuce). Fresh fruit.
*Tea*: wholemeal bread and Marmite, nuts and raisins, lemon tea.
*Supper*: vegetable stew with jacket potatoes. Apricot tart with coconut cream. A fruit drink before bedtime.

Children's meals

| HOW | WHY |
| --- | --- |
| 1. Give large amounts of body-building foods (proteins and minerals). | For growth of body tissue and bone. |
| 2. Supply children with sufficient energy-giving foods. | To supply energy for rapid growth and physical activity. |
| 3. Give plenty of the vitamin foods, fresh fruit, dairy foods, orange juice. | Vitamin deficiency is serious in young children, their growth and development are arrested. |
| 4. Give sweet foods at end of meal only, and avoid constant eating of sweets between meals. | To satisfy appetite only after essential nutrients have been supplied. |
| 5. Give a large variety of foods. | To encourage children to eat different foods and to stop them being 'choosy'. |
| 6. Arrange for meals to be at regular times and in a happy atmosphere. | To encourage regular eating habits and to help digestion. |
| 7. Include some crisp food, e.g. raw apple. | To exercise jaws and strengthen teeth. |
| 8. Be sure that the child has at least 500 ml of milk each day. | To ensure the supply of essential nutrients. |

*A typical day's menu for a child under 5 years:*
*Breakfast*: cereal or porridge, with milk and sugar. Scrambled, boiled or poached egg. Bread and butter and milk.
*Mid-morning*: orange juice.
*Dinner*: stewed meat or steamed fish, mashed potatoes, a green vegetable. Milk pudding with stewed fruit or lemon mousse, using evaporated milk in place of cream.
*Tea*: sandwiches of watercress, or cheese and tomato. Wholemeal bread and butter, honey, a piece of cake.
*Bedtime*: raw apple or carrot. Milk drink.

Meals for invalids and convalescents

Obey the instructions of the doctor with regard to feeding, but the following rules will be found generally useful:

| HOW | WHY |
| --- | --- |
| 1. Give plenty of foods supplying proteins and minerals. | Loss of weight during illness must be made good. |
| 2. Give plenty of fluids and vitamin foods. | To replace body fluid lost in illness, and to aid body repair. |

| | |
|---|---|
| 3. Have suitable drinks always available. | Patient is often thirsty. |
| 4. Make food attractive and as colourful as possible. | To tempt the appetite. |
| 5. Be very particular about cleanliness in preparation and serving. | To avoid any further infection. |
| 6. Choose foods which are light, nourishing and easily digested (steamed or grilled rather than fried). | Appetite and digestion are both poor after illness. |
| 7. Give small meals at frequent intervals rather than large meals. | Patients will be encouraged to eat more. |
| 8. Avoid all highly spiced or over-seasoned food. | Patients usually dislike strong flavours. |
| 9. Avoid letting the smell of food during preparation reach the sickroom. | Invalids usually dislike the smell of cooking. |

*Note.* Milk drinks may be reinforced with eggs or patent foods. Fruit drinks may be sweetened with glucose. Lightly boiled eggs, egg custards, creamed fish or chicken and cream soups are all digestible and nourishing.

*A typical day's menu for a convalescent patient who has had influenza:*
*Breakfast*: fresh fruit juice, lightly boiled egg, thin bread and butter, marmalade, weak tea or coffee.
*Mid-morning*: a milk drink and a biscuit.
*Dinner*: baked white fish and parsley sauce, creamed potatoes and grilled tomatoes. Milk pudding or a light sponge pudding.
*Tea*: wholemeal bread and butter. Honey, Marmite or tomato sandwich. Tea to drink.
*Supper*: creamed soup, steamed lamb chop, mashed carrot or sieved green vegetable. Egg custard, fresh fruit.
*Bedtime*: milk drink.

## Packed meals

| **HOW** | **WHY** |
|---|---|
| 1. Try to plan a well-balanced meal to include foods containing some protein and vitamins. | It is easy to include too much carbohydrate as bread and pastry. |
| 2. Avoid having food too dry, i.e. use moist fillings for sandwiches. | It is difficult to eat dry food. |
| 3. Include something to drink, preferably carried in a vacuum flask. | It can be kept hot or cold. |

| | |
|---|---|
| 4. Prepare food easy to pack. | For cleanliness and convenience. |
| 5. Pack food carefully, using containers, polythene bags, etc. | To protect it and prevent it from drying. |

*Suggestions for packed meals:*
1. Sandwiches: of cheese, meat, ham or eggs. Pasties containing meat, fish, cheese and vegetables. Small pork pies or sausage rolls. Scotch eggs. Individual quiches or flans. Meat loaf or pâté. Crispbread biscuits with cream cheese and watercress. Any salad vegetables, packed in a plastic container.
2. Biscuits or shortbread, or any non-crumbly cake. Fruit turnovers, mince pies or jam tarts. Fresh fruit. A bar of chocolate. Nuts. Mousse or fruit salad in plastic containers.
3. Tea, coffee or hot soup in a vacuum flask. Fruit drink in a bottle. Cold milk in a bottle.

*Hints on making sandwiches:*
*Note.* Use a really sharp knife for cutting bread.
1. Use a loaf at least one day old or, if obtainable, use thinly sliced bread. (The usual sliced loaf is often too thickly cut.)
2. Cream the butter or the margarine before spreading. Warm it slightly if necessary.
3. Spread the fat evenly.
4. Be generous with the filling, which should be fairly moist and well seasoned.
5. Experiment with fillings, e.g. grated apple and sultanas, chutney mixed with grated cheese.
6. Press the sandwiches firmly and, if intended for invalids or for a special occasion, cut off the crusts very thinly.
7. Wrap immediately in waxed paper, cling film or in a polythene bag.
8. Serve neatly garnished with a little watercress, lettuce or tomato.

## Meals for special occasions

| HOW | WHY |
|---|---|
| 1. Take care to have balanced meals. | It is easy to serve too much carbohydrate and insufficient main foods, vegetables and fruits. |
| 2. Give both sweet and savoury dishes, and vary the flavour, colour and texture. | To suit all tastes. |
| 3. Serve hot and cold foods. | Variety is interesting. Cold foods can be prepared in advance. |
| 4. Pay special attention to layout and serving. Be skilful with decorations and garnishes. | This can emphasise the reason for the party, e.g. with a centre-piece of birthday cake. |

5. Include drinks; preferably both hot and cold.

6. For a buffet meal, choose food which can be easily eaten while standing.

Child's birthday party

Choose simple familiar dishes and present them attractively. Choose something from each of the following groups:
1. Birthday cake (this may be a simple Victoria sandwich appropriately iced), small iced cakes, jam tarts, éclairs, small biscuits, meringues, etc.
2. Small sausage rolls, cheese straws, cheese scones, savoury sandwiches.
3. Small sticks of carrot, celery or cucumber.
4. Buttered buns, scones, bread and butter.
5. Jelly, ice-cream, fruit salad, instant whip or mousse.
6. Milk, milk shakes, fruit drinks, Coca-Cola, or tea.

Suggestions for indoor buffet parties

1. Sausage rolls, savoury pasties, small meat pies, savoury flans, cheese straws, cheese scones, vol-au-vent cases with savoury fillings. Savoury sandwiches, or small rolls with a savoury filling. Small cooked sausages on sticks. Salad cut small with a salad dressing. Cold chicken joints.
2. Small iced cakes, éclairs, meringues, vanilla slices, biscuits of all kinds.
3. Jellies, trifles, mousses, creams, fruit salad, ice-cream, etc.
4. Coffee, tea and cold fruit drinks.

Suggestions for parties outdoors

1. Fried sausages, tomatoes, and mushrooms, hamburgers, 'hot dogs', potatoes baked in jackets, toasted sandwiches, 'cheese dreams'.
2. Doughnuts, gingerbread, small cakes, biscuits.
3. Soup, coffee, fruit drinks, Coca-Cola, etc.

Suggestions for tea and coffee parties

1. For tea parties, serve thin bread and butter (white and wholemeal), buttered scones (plain or cheese), filled sandwiches or bridge rolls, cakes, biscuits and tea.
2. For morning coffee parties, serve biscuits, buns or small cakes, and coffee, with hot milk served separately.

**Economy in catering**

The general rule is to try to buy the correct amount for the number of people to be catered for, and thus to avoid having left-over food.
(See notes on economy when shopping page 63 and economy of fuel page 71.)

**Table showing approximate amounts needed for each person**

| | |
|---|---|
| 1. *MEAT* | |
| Chops, cutlets | One |
| Stewing meat | 100 g |
| Meat with bone | 150 g |
| Joint for roasting or boiling | 100–150 g |
| (A joint needs to be at least a kilo in weight to be cooked satisfactorily.) | |
| Sausages | 100 g |
| Cooked cold meat | 75–100 g |
| 2. *FISH* | |
| Fillets | 100 g |
| Cutlets, including weight of bone | 150 g |
| Small whole fish, such as herring, mackerel | One |
| 3. *VEGETABLES* | |
| Potatoes – old | 200 g |
| – new | 150 g |
| Green vegetables | 100–150 g |
| Carrots and other roots | 100 g |
| French or runner beans | 100 g |
| Garden peas in pods | 100 g |
| Tomatoes | 50–75 g |
| Dried peas or other pulses | 25 g |
| Watercress | 25 g |
| 4. *FRUIT* | |
| Stewing fruit | 100 g |
| Dried fruit | 40 g |
| 5. *SOUP* | 125–250 ml |
| 6. *CHEESE* | 40 g |
| 7. *MILK PUDDING* | 175 ml |
| 8. *PUDDINGS*, steamed or boiled | 40 g flour |
| *PASTRY* for tarts, etc. | 40 g flour |
| 9. *CUSTARDS* | 125 ml |
| 10. *SAUCES AND GRAVIES* | 60 ml |

## Left-over food

If food is left over after a meal, it should be kept clean and covered in a cold place. This will prevent spoilage or contamination by micro-organisms. Dishes made from previously cooked food are known as *réchauffé* or re-heated dishes. The following points must be considered if re-heated food is to be palatable, digestible and safe:

*Réchauffé* food

| HOW | WHY |
|---|---|
| 1. Before being re-heated, meat and fish must be well seasoned and flavoured. | Re-cooked food can be insipid. |
| 2. It must be moistened with a good gravy or sauce. | Re-cooked food is usually dry. |
| 3. Some foods require a protective covering, e.g. egg and breadcrumbs on croquettes. | To prevent further drying during cooking. |
| 4. All ingredients must be pre-cooked. | To reduce re-heating time. |
| 5. Food must be finely cut or minced. | |
| 6. Food must be re-heated thoroughly, but only for a short time. | To destroy bacteria, but long re-heating hardens all proteins. |
| 7. Do not give re-heated foods to infants or invalids. | They are less digestible than freshly cooked foods and may have lost vitamins B and C. |
| 8. Always serve with some protective foods, e.g. salads, fresh green vegetables or fruit. | To provide the vitamins destroyed by re-heating. |
| 9. Never re-heat any dish more than once. | Nearly all flavour will be lost. |

Uses for left-over food

1. *Cold meat*: shepherd's pie, mince, rissoles, croquettes, meat pasties, curries, stuffed vegetables, risotto.
2. *Cold fish*: fish and potato pie, Russian fish pie, fish pasties, fish cakes, fish salad, soufflés.
3. *Potatoes*: sauté potatoes, bubble and squeak, fish pie, shepherd's pie, potato salad.
4. *Fat from meat*: clarify and use for frying.
5. *Stale cheese*: grate and use in cheese pastry, cheese savouries, sauces and soups.
6. *Sour milk*: cottage cheese, scones.
7. *Stale bread*: white crumbs for stuffings, steamed puddings, cheese pudding, coating fish. Crusts may be baked slowly and either used as rusks or crushed and used as browned crumbs.
8. *Stale cake*: trifles, queen of puddings or refrigerator flans.
9. *Egg yolks*: for coating, for biscuit making or, when scrambled, for sandwich fillings.

*Economy in the use of fuel*

How to save fuel

1. Save oven fuel by:
a) Cooking whole meal in oven, e.g. stew in casserole, together with potatoes in jackets and baked fruit pie.
b) Cooking together the dishes for several meals, e.g. cakes, flan cases, casserole dishes.
2. Save fuel on the hotplate by:
a) Standing several saucepans on one plate or burner (a set of triangular pans is economical).
b) Using a three-tiered steamer for whole meal, e.g. for steak and kidney pudding, cauliflower, potatoes, and stewed fruit in covered dish; all at the same time.
c) Using a pressure cooker which greatly reduces cooking time and therefore uses less fuel.
d) Cooking potatoes in a steamer over boiling root vegetables.
3. Fuel can be saved in all cases by not turning the gas or electricity higher than necessary, and by turning it off soon as it is no longer needed.
4. A grill uses a lot of fuel and is not very versatile, so try to avoid this.
5. Serve some uncooked foods, e.g. salads.

**Time planning**

Besides being able to choose, prepare and cook well-balanced and attractive meals, the cook must be able to serve them punctually. How to do this requires thought and organisation, e.g. a housewife needs to prepare a meal for herself, her husband and two school age children. It must be served at 12.45 pm to fit in with her husband's lunch hour and the children's school hours.

Planned menu

Beef and tomato casserole, boiled potatoes, green vegetable.
Stewed fruit and baked egg custard.
1. The cost of the meal fits into the family budget. It is economical on fuel, as it is mainly cooked in the oven.
2. It is nutritionally well-balanced and liked by the family.
3. The preparation time allows the housewife time for other work or leisure activity during the morning.
4. The menu is flexible, and the main course can be re-heated in the evening if the husband is unable to reach home at lunch time. Tinned or frozen peas can then replace the fresh green vegetable and the second course can be served cold.

Ingredients required

*From store*: dripping, flour, mixed herbs, salt, pepper, stock cube, egg, tin of tomatoes, milk, sugar.
*To buy*: 500 g stewing beef, onions, plums or other fruit in season, potatoes, cabbage.

Casserole recipe

| *Ingredients:* | *Method:* |
|---|---|
| 500 g stewing steak.<br>2 level tblsp flour.<br>Salt, pepper, mixed herbs.<br>25 g dripping.<br>2 large onions.<br>Small tin tomatoes.<br>Stock cube dissolved in<br>375 ml boiling water. | Cut meat into cubes, coat in seasoned flour. Peel and chop onions. Brown meat and onions in dripping. Place all ingredients in covered casserole in a slow oven until meat is tender. Taste for seasoning adding more if necessary. |

Time required for dishes

| *Dish* | *Preparation time* | *Cooking time* |
|---|---|---|
| Casserole | ½ hour | 2 hours |
| Boiled potatoes | 5–10 minutes | 20 minutes |
| Cabbage | 5 minutes | 10 minutes |
| Stewed fruit | 5–10 minutes | 40 minutes (in oven) |
| Egg custard | 10 minutes | 45 minutes |
| *Dishing up time* | 5 minutes | |

From this it is obvious that the dishes needing the longest cooking time must be prepared first. The work should begin at 10.15 am.

Time plan

| | |
|---|---|
| 10.15 am | Collect equipment and ingredients, prepare meat and onions, make stock, open tin of tomatoes. |
| 10.30 am | Pre-heat oven 150°C (Gas 2). Place ingredients in casserole. |
| 10.45 am | Put casserole in oven. Prepare egg custard. Wash up dishes. |
| 11 am | Break for an hour until 12 noon. |
| 12 noon | Stand custard dish in a dish of water (bain-marie). Put custard into oven. Place fruit with a little water and sugar to taste into another casserole, cover and put in oven. |
| 12.15 pm | Prepare potatoes and put to boil. Boil water for cabbage, and prepare cabbage. |
| 12.30 pm | Put cabbage to boil in boiling salted water.<br>Lay the table.<br>Tidy kitchen.<br>Dish vegetables as they are cooked. |
| 12.45 pm | Serve the meal. |

# 8 Cookery for practical examinations

*Aims  Understanding the question  Planning, the choice of dishes, order or work, ingredients required  Examination day*

**Aims**

1. To show off practical cookery skills.
2. To choose correct type of food for the occasion or question.
3. To prepare well-balanced meals.
4. To serve foods attractively.

Most practical examinations are arranged in two parts. First you are given a question or 'situation' for which you must plan to cook certain dishes or a meal that is suitable for the occasion. Details of your chosen menu, a time plan and a shopping list must be written out and submitted to the examiner or teacher. Secondly a few days later, you are required to cook these dishes, carefully following your plan, and present them attractively to the examiner.

Pre-exam preparation

*Cookery skills*: you will have learnt the correct methods of preparing, cooking and serving all the important types of dishes. As you work through the course you should keep a list of recipes used under different headings, e.g. meat, cheese, fish and egg dishes, vegetarian, low kilocalorie, invalid dishes, hot and cold puddings, cakes, biscuits – you can think of more headings. You should have a record of the recipe using quantities for 3–4 people, with notes on size of tins, temperature and time for baking, correct serving, decorating or garnishing. Make notes of suitable accompaniments, e.g. pizza with a green salad and French dressing.

You will learn to appreciate that some dishes require more skill to make than others. If you are going to 'show off' your ability to cook, some of these must be included in a practical test. Here are some ideas for skilful dishes: most types of baking – pastries, cakes, yeast doughs or biscuits; meat dishes such as casseroles where colour, seasoning, thickening and appearance are so important; roast meat with all the correct accompaniments; fish Mornay with a border of piped potato; flans and gateaux with glazed fruit and piped cream; glacé and butter icings on a decorated cake; a cold soufflé using gelatine.

However you will not have time to cook five very skilful or complicated dishes but should try to include two or three according to the type of question. The other dishes may include grapefruit or a soup with toasted croutons, freshly cooked vegetables, fresh lemonade or coffee made from ground coffee beans.

You will not gain good marks by planning only a few skilful dishes: you should aim to have plenty of food on the table at the end of the test, e.g. about 5 items and a drink in two-and-a-quarter hours.

## Understanding the question

Cookery terms used in the exam paper

Each word in the question is important and will have a special meaning. The following definitions may be helpful:

A *meal*: will consist of two or three courses depending on time, cost and occasion. A meal may have grapefruit or soup, followed by a main dish accompanied by vegetables and bread rolls; then a sweet and a drink. Do serve a drink with *all* meals.

A *dish*: either a soup, or a main protein dish or, possibly, a pudding where several ingredients are used to make a main item as distinct from an accompaniment. A dish with suitable accompaniments will make one course of a meal. (A dish also means the plate on which food is served.)

*Accompaniments*: the following are examples of accompaniments which might be served with a variety of dishes: bread rolls, potatoes, rice, vegetables, salads with a dressing, savoury or sweet sauces, shortbread fingers. For instance, spaghetti Bolognese as a main dish can be accompanied by bread rolls and a green salad with French dressing. (*Note.* Boiled potatoes and Brussels sprouts are not suitable accompaniments for this Italian style dish!)

A *choice* of dishes means that at least two must be served.

A *selection* of dishes implies more than two items. Sometimes it is possible to make more than one item from a batch, e.g. 250 g bread dough will make a pizza and some bread rolls or Chelsea buns.

At a *buffet meal* the food should be served in such a way that it is easy to eat either with the fingers, or by using a fork or spoon while holding the plate.

A *beverage* is the correct name for a drink.

(The whole of Chapter 7 on Meal Planning is very relevant to choosing the correct dishes for meals on various occasions.)

## Planning for the exam

Planning

When you first see the question you need to spend quite some time making the correct choice of dishes. When you have an outline of the five or so dishes you intend to make check the following points:

1. Have you 'shown off' your cookery skills? Is there plenty of work to do in the time available? Or is there so much work that you will be too rushed?

2. Is there variety of colour, flavour, texture and cooking methods?
3. Are there some hot and some cold dishes?
4. What oven temperatures and times are needed? Can you cook all the items you have selected?
5. Check that you have read the whole of the question and satisfied all the conditions.

You must write down the names of the dishes you intend to cook, in menu order, and indicate the quantities of ingredients you will use. Do plan enough work to keep really busy otherwise your marks may be rather low.

Next plan your order of work and give an outline of the method you intend to use. This may be set out as shown in the time plan on page 71. Remember to cook cakes early in the test if you want them to cool before icing. Start flaky pastry early to allow time to rest.

Lastly, you may have to write out a shopping list. Start at the beginning of your list of ingredients and go through systematically, adding up the total quantity of each food. Do not forget to order garnishes such as watercress, tomato, parsley or lettuce. Certain foods may be ordered pre-prepared, e.g. stock, grated cheese, or cold cooked meat for *réchauffé* dishes.

**Examination day**

Points to remember

What will the examiner be looking for? To see that you are a well organised and skilful cook.

Some marks may be given for personal appearance and you can gain full marks here. Check that you have clean, short fingernails with no nail varnish. Your hair should be clean and neatly tied back so that it does not fall over your face. You should have a clean apron, marked clearly with your name to assist the examiner.

The table on which you serve your food should have a freshly laundered cloth, a small arrangement of flowers and a card with your name, question number and the menu or list of dishes. You must choose the dishes on which you serve the food carefully. Use the correct style of serving dish and use sweet and savoury doilys where necessary.

Arrive in good time for the start of the examination. You need time to collect all the dishes, equipment and ingredients that you need. You must check the regulations of the examination, usually you are not allowed to weigh out the ingredients or light the oven before the start of the examination.

During the examination, keep your work table tidy, having on it only the things you are using. When you have finished with a pan or a plate, put it on the draining board and try to wash up two or three times during the test so that you do not create a mountain of pans! As you finish the cooking, remember to warm the serving dishes and keep food hot. Serve all hot dishes at the end of the examination, just as you would for a meal. Cold dishes can be set on your serving table as you finish them.

If you have an accident and burn something or drop it, try to rectify your mistake using your common sense. Do not throw it out in disgust if it can possibly be 'saved'. Food which is edible should be put on the serving table even if you are disappointed with it: you will gain *some* marks if you do this. Serve all unfinished items too, there are no marks for items which are not on the table at the end of the test.

# 9 Cooking

*Why we cook food    How heat is applied    Methods of cooking*

## Why we cook food

Cooking may be defined as the heating of food to bring about both physical and chemical changes.

Aims in cooking food

1. *To make it safe to consume*
Milk is sterilised or pasteurised to destroy organisms of disease and to reduce the number of milk-souring bacteria.

Pork should always be well cooked to destroy any Salmonellae bacteria or cysts of tape-worm which may be present.

Drinking water should be boiled if not obtained from a reliable source and known to be pure.

2. *To make it easier to swallow and to digest*
Starch grains swell when heated, and gelatinise so that the digestive juices can more easily penetrate them.

The cellulose fibres and cell walls of fruit and vegetables are softened.

The connective tissue around the muscle fibres of meat softens because the protein in it (collagen) is changed to gelatine.

3. *To make it more attractive and appetising*
The appearance of a well browned cake is more attractive than that of the dough from which it is made.

The smell of cooking can stimulate the appetite.

4. *To introduce variety in the diet*
Food can be cooked in various ways, e.g. eggs can be scrambled, boiled, poached, etc.

Flavours can be combined together such as those of meat, vegetables, seasoning and herbs in savoury dishes.

5. *To preserve food for later use*
Fruit may be bottled or made into jam.

## How heat is applied

Heat is essential for cooking. It may be passed from a heat source to the food by three basic methods – radiation, conduction, convection; or more often by a mixture of these three methods. In microwave heating, the source of heat is formed within the food being cooked.

Radiation

Heat passes from its source in direct rays until it falls on an object in its path. Grilling makes use of radiated heat, heat is also radiated from the top and sides of a hot oven.

*Radiation*

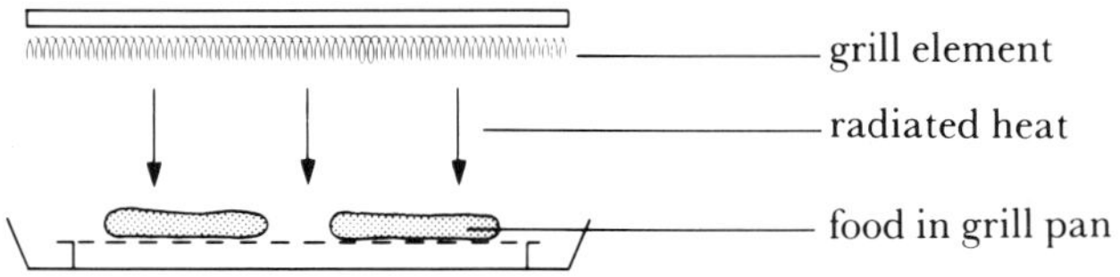


*Infra-red radiation*: infra-red grills produce more rays in the infra-red or long wave-length than traditional grills. These rays are better absorbed by the food and so it cooks more quickly.

---

Conduction

Heat passes through two solids in contact. Heat passes from a hotplate through the base of a metal saucepan and good contact is necessary for efficient transfer of heat.

*Conduction*

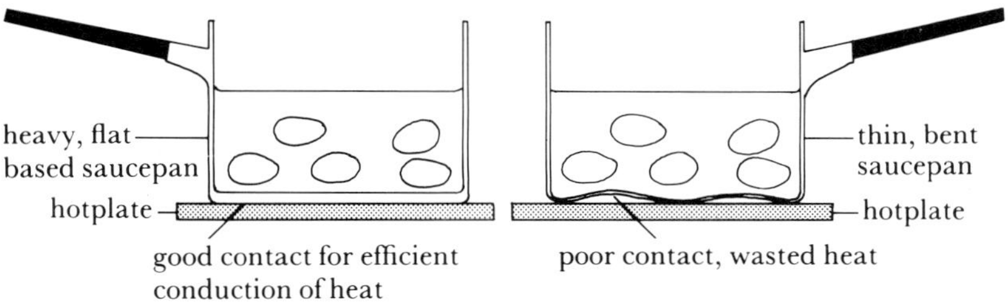


Heat passes from the outside of a joint of meat to the centre by conduction. Some materials conduct heat quickly, e.g. metal; some do not, e.g. wood. For this reason use a wooden spoon to stir a sauce so that you do not burn your fingers on the spoon.

---

Convection

Heat is transferred by the movement of heated particles of gases or liquids. On heating the particles expand, they become less dense and rise. The cooler particles sink to take their place thus causing convection currents which distribute heat. Ovens are heated by convection currents. Heat is distributed through the liquid contents of a pan by convection currents.

*Convection*

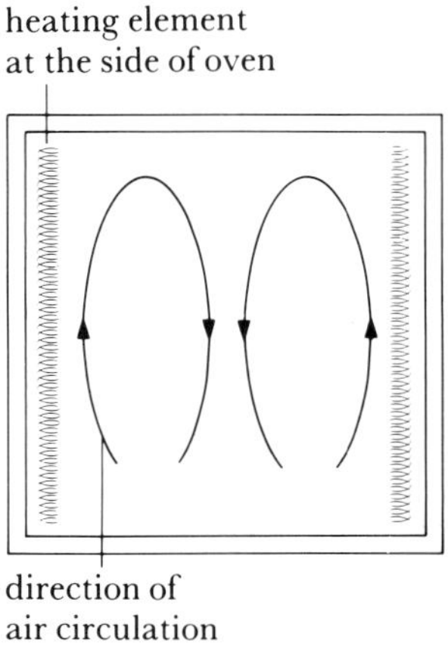

Microwave heating

Heat is generated within the food as opposed to traditional methods of cooking where heat is transferred from an outside source. Microwaves are non-ionising electromagnetic waves like radio and television waves. They may be reflected, e.g. by metal; transmitted, e.g. by glass and china; and then absorbed, e.g. by water. The water in food absorbs the electromagnetic energy and it is converted to heat energy. So the water in the food becomes hot and the food is cooked.

**Methods of cooking**

'Dry' methods of cookery are baking, roasting, frying and grilling. 'Wet' methods of cookery are boiling, stewing and steaming. All these methods use water. Braising is a combination of stewing and baking.

Grilling

Grilling is a dry method of cooking by means of heat radiated from a heated grill, or from a smokeless fire.

*Foods suitable for grilling:*

1. Small, usually expensive cuts of meat, e.g. fillet or rump steak, lamb or pork chops and cutlets.
2. Sausages, kidneys, liver, bacon rashers, fish fingers.
3. Whole small fish, e.g. herrings, mackerel, or fillets and cutlets of larger fish.
4. Tomatoes, mushrooms.

*Advantages*: food is quickly cooked, tasty, and there is no loss of soluble nutrients.
*Disadvantages*: only suitable for the more tender and therefore more expensive cuts of meat. Needs considerable skill to do well.

| HOW | WHY |
|---|---|
| 1. Brush food with fat or oil unless it contains fat. | To prevent charring. |
| 2. See that the grill is really hot before beginning to cook. | To seal the outside protein of the food and so prevent loss of juices. To brown toast quickly and prevent drying. |
| 3. Turn food frequently using tongs or two spoons (not forks). | To ensure that food is cooked evenly and to prevent loss of juices. |
| 4. Serve quickly, without gravy, usually with chipped or sauté potatoes, tomatoes and mushrooms. | Food correctly grilled should be moist with its own juices. |
| 5. Serve a suitable sauce, e.g. with steak, serve *maître d'hôtel* butter. | To add flavour and to increase food value. |

## Frying

Frying is the cooking of food in hot fat or oil usually between 180°C–205°C.

*Fats suitable for frying:*
1. They should be clean and free from specks from previous frying which spoil the appearance of the food.
2. They should be free from moisture, as the cooking temperature required cannot be reached until all the water is driven off.
3. They should be free from any strong taste which might spoil the food.
4. They should have a high decomposition temperature so that they do not burn easily.

They may be oils, e.g. sunflower, soya or corn oils, or fats, e.g. lard, cooking fats or clarified dripping. Butter may, on occasion, be used in shallow frying for good flavour. Mix it with a little vegetable oil to prevent burning.

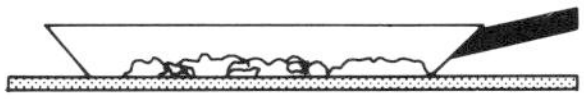

*Dry frying for fatty food*

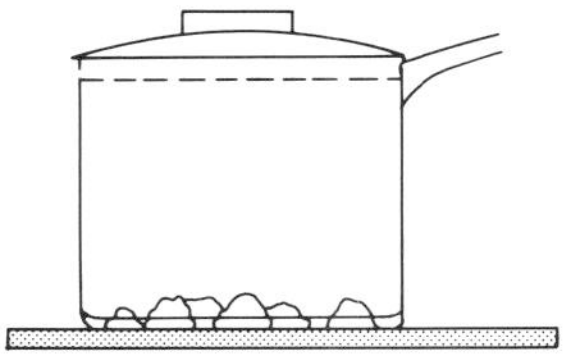

*Sauté frying in a pan with the lid on, using a little fat*

*Foods suitable for frying:*
1. *For dry frying*: food containing fat, such as bacon, sausages, herrings. The fat melts and runs out of the food.
2. *For sautéing*: foods which will absorb melted fat, such as potatoes, kidneys and vegetables for soup making.
3. *For shallow frying*: foods which may be cooked in heated fat covering the bottom of the pan, e.g. eggs, cutlets, fish.
4. *For deep frying*: foods which can be cooked in sufficient fat to cover them, e.g. doughnuts, fish in batter.

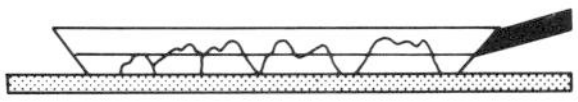

*Shallow frying with hot fat covering the bottom of the pan*

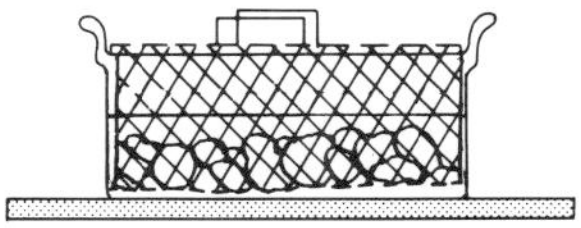

*Deep frying with enough fat to cover the food, using a removable wire basket*

Some foods require a coating before frying, such as seasoned flour or oatmeal; a batter of flour and milk, with or without egg; or egg and breadcrumbs. This coating prevents loss of flavour, juices and nutrients and improves the appearance of the food, preventing it falling apart.

*Advantages of frying*: fried food is quickly cooked and tasty, with no loss of soluble nutrients. It increases the energy value of the food.
*Disadvantages*: frying is only suitable for the more expensive cuts of meat, needs skill and is dangerous unless done carefully – the fat may catch fire, particularly in deep fat frying. Fried food is not easily digested.

| HOW | WHY |
|---|---|
| 1. Have fat absolutely clean. | Otherwise the appearance of the food is spoilt. |
| 2. Have fat at correct temperature. When hot enough it should be still, without bubbles or smoke. Use a thermometer. | All the water has been driven off, but fat has not reached decomposition point. Food can be cooked at correct temperature for correct time. |

| | |
|---|---|
| 3. Coat the outside of the food before deep frying. | To prevent the escape of juices and to prevent the food becoming soggy. |
| 4. Do not fry too much food at once. | Temperature of fat is then lowered and food spoilt. |
| 5. Turn food during shallow frying, and during deep frying if it floats, e.g. doughnuts. Turn the food carefully. | To ensure even cooking. To avoid breaking up the food and scratching linings of non-stick pans. |
| 6. Carefully drain fried food, if possible on kitchen paper. | To remove excess fat and to prevent food being soggy. |

## Roasting

Roasting really means cooking by radiated heat on a spit; it is also used to mean cooking in fat in the oven. This form of roasting is, of course, a type of baking.

*Foods suitable for roasting*:

1. Better cuts of meat, e.g. sirloin or rib of beef, leg or shoulder of lamb, leg or loin of pork.
2. Young poultry of all kinds.
3. Vegetables such as potatoes and parsnips, which can be cooked in the fat with the meat.

*Advantages*: appearance of food is usually good. Food is tasty and retains its full flavour and food value.
*Disadvantages*: needs attention and basting, or the food will be dry and hard. Only the tender and therefore expensive cuts of meat are suitable.

| HOW | WHY |
|---|---|
| 1. Weigh and wipe the meat. | To be able to calculate the cooking time and to clean the meat. |
| 2. Dust with seasoned flour. | To make a crisp tasty outside to the joint. |
| 3. Have ready a large tin containing previously heated fat (lard or dripping). The tin may be covered or open. Place meat in tin. | To develop the flavour of meat, and prevent loss of nutrients. The hot fat ensures a crisp outside coating. |
| 4. *Either* put into hot oven at about 230°C (Gas 8) for 20 minutes and then reduce to 180°C (Gas 4) for rest of time. | To seal the outside protein. |
| *Or* place in a moderate oven at about 150°C (Gas 2) and cook slowly for about twice as long. | To cook slowly and thus to soften the connective tissue if meat tends to be tough. |
| *Or* put it in a cold oven which is then heated to 200°C (Gas 7). | |

| | |
|---|---|
| 5. If uncovered, baste frequently. | To keep meat moist and to prevent shrinkage. |
| 6. Dish up when cooked and serve with gravy made from the meat juices left in the pan after pouring off the fat. | To avoid waste of flavour and of nutrients. |

*Cooking times for roasting in a hot oven*:
Beef: allow 15 minutes per 500 g and 15 minutes extra.
Lamb: allow 20 minutes per 500 g and 20 minutes extra.
Pork: allow 25 minutes per 500 g and 25 minutes extra.
Chicken: allow 20 minutes per 500 g and 20 minutes extra.

## Baking

Baking is a dry method of cookery in which food is cooked in an oven which may be pre-heated to the required temperature, usually between 95°C and 260°C (Gas ¼–9).

*Foods suitable for baking*:
1. Meat (see roasting).
2. Whole fish or large cutlets.
3. Vegetables, e.g. potatoes, onions (not green vegetables).
4. Pastry, cakes, yeast mixtures etc.

*Advantages*: there is no loss of soluble nutrients. Food does not break up, but keeps its shape. Food has an attractive appearance.
*Disadvantages*: requires attention, otherwise food may burn. It is expensive to heat the oven, and therefore wasteful to bake only one dish.

*Baking of flour mixtures*
The rules vary with different mixtures and these will be dealt with in Chapter 10.

*Baking of fish*

| **HOW** | **WHY** |
|---|---|
| 1. Prepare and wash fish. Stuff if desired. | To clean it and to add extra flavour. |
| 2. Place in greased dish, cover with small dabs of fat, season and cover with greased paper. | To keep fish moist during cooking. |
| 3. Bake at about 180°C (Gas 4) for approximately 10 minutes per 500 g until flesh is just opaque (protein coagulated). Do not overcook. | Otherwise it will be dry. |

*Baking of vegetables*: e.g. potatoes, tomatoes, onions, stuffed peppers.

| HOW | WHY |
|---|---|
| 1. Wash well. Cook in skins if possible. | To avoid loss of food value. |
| 2. Prick skins of potatoes. | To prevent bursting due to generation of steam. |
| Do not prick beetroot. | To prevent loss of colour. |
| 3. Cook in moderate oven until tender. | Useful when whole meal is cooked in oven. |

Boiling

Boiling is a method of cooking carried out in liquid at a temperature of 100°C. In practice it is usually done in a covered pan – meat and vegetables together. Boiling is a moist method and therefore softens tough cuts of meat.

*Foods suitable for boiling*:
1. Large joints of medium quality meat, either fresh or salted, e.g. silverside, brisket, ox tongue, ham.
2. Large fish, e.g. salmon, cod, hake.
3. All vegetables and pulses.
4. Flour mixtures, e.g. dumplings.
5. Soups, stocks.

*Advantages*: it is a simple method and requires little attention. It is economical of fuel, as a whole course may be cooked in the same pan – meat and vegetable together. Boiling is a moist method and therefore softens tough cuts of meat.
*Disadvantages*: loss of soluble nutrients in the water. Food often looks unattractive. Food may break into pieces during cooking. It is a rather long, slow method.

Steaming

Steaming is a moist method of cooking by steam from boiling liquid. Steaming may be either by direct contact between the food and the steam, as in a steamer, or by indirect contact. In the latter method, the steam reaches only the container, as when the food is in a covered basin or between two plates.

*Foods suitable for steaming*:
1. Small pieces of meat, e.g. chops, cutlets, liver.
2. Small fish or fillets, e.g. whiting, cod steaks.
3. Root vegetables and potatoes, but not green vegetables.
4. Fresh and dried fruit.
5. Puddings, suet pastry, batter mixtures, egg custards.

*Advantages*: no loss of nutrients, or flavour. No fat is added so the food remains light and easily digested and therefore suitable for infants and invalids. Economical of fuel, as the whole meal can

be cooked on one burner. Needs little attention except to see that the water does not boil away or come off the boil. Food remains whole and is not broken up.
*Disadvantages*: it is a lengthy process. Dishes are sometimes unattractive in appearance unless skill is used in dishing up. Sauces and garnishes are required.

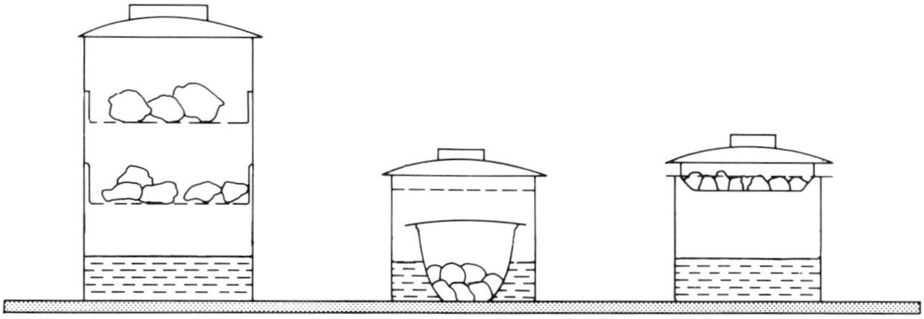

*1 Tiered steamer. Each tier has a perforated base and the bottom one fits on to a pan of boiling water*

*2 Covered basin standing in a pan of boiling water*

*3 Plate covered with a lid, standing over a pan of boiling water*

| HOW | WHY |
| --- | --- |
| 1. Food should be steamed either: a) in a steamer b) in a covered basin standing in boiling water c) between two plates over a pan of boiling water. | |
| The lid of the steamer must always fit tightly and the water must always be boiling. | To prevent loss of steam and to keep temperature constant. |
| 2. Add boiling water to pan when necessary during cooking. | To keep up a constant supply of steam. |
| 3. Cover the food or wrap it in greased paper or metal foil. | To prevent loss of juices during cooking, and to prevent foods from becoming sodden. |

Pressure cooking

It must be stressed that it is very important indeed to follow exactly the instructions given by the manufacturer of the pressure cooker.

Pressure cooking is cooking by superheated steam in a closed vessel with a strong and firmly secured lid with safety valve. As the steam cannot easily escape, the pressure is increased inside the cooker, and the liquid boils at a higher temperature. With many makes of pressure cooker the pressure is increased by adding a series of valve weights. The higher the pressure, the greater the temperature and the shorter the cooking time. The corresponding rise of temperature with pressure is as follows:

| *Pressure* | *°C at which water boils* |
|---|---|
| 1.05 $kg/cm^2$ (atmospheric pressure) | 100°C |
| Additional 0.35 $kg/cm^2$ | 108°C |
| Additional 0.7 $kg/cm^2$ | 112°C |
| Additional 1.05 $kg/cm^2$ | 120°C |

*Advantages*: very quick method. Tough coarse foods can be softened easily and quickly. Very economical of fuel. No loss of nutrients.
*Disadvantages*: needs skill and experience. There is danger from careless handling of pressure cookers.

*How to use a pressure cooker*

| HOW | WHY |
|---|---|
| 1. Put a small amount of water into the cooker. | Very little is needed, as steam does not escape. |
| 2. Put in food. Do not overcrowd cooker. | This allows room for steam. |
| 3. Put on lid with valve open and heat for a few minutes. | To drive out the air. |
| 4. Close valve and heat until valve hisses, or until dial shows correct pressure. | To build up the pressure. |
| 5. Reduce the heat and start timing the cooking. | Required pressure and temperature are reached. |
| 6. After given time, cool the cooker. Then carefully open the valve and then open the cooker. | This reduces pressure inside cooker to that of the atmosphere. |

*Pressure cooker*

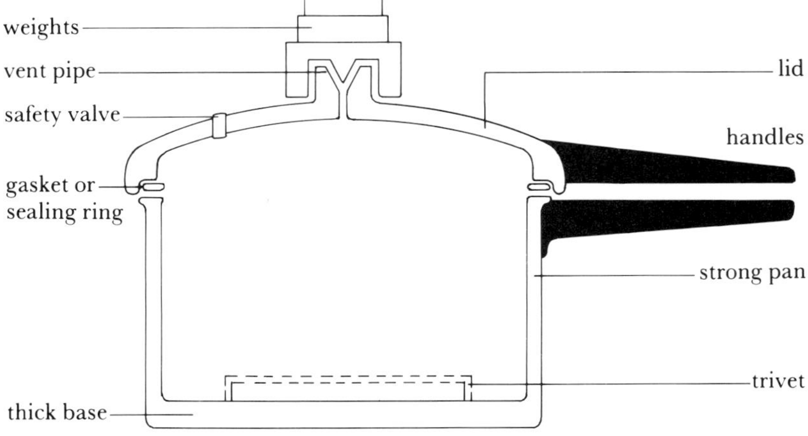

## Stewing

Stewing is a long slow method of cooking food in a small quantity of liquid, at a temperature just below boiling point. This can be carried out in a tightly covered pan on top of the cooker, or in a covered casserole in the oven.

*Foods suitable for stewing*:
1. Fresh and dried fruits.
2. All vegetables except green ones.
3. Cheaper, coarser cuts of meat, e.g. shin of beef, scrag end or breast of lamb.

*Advantages*: makes appetising and attractive dishes from cheaper cuts of meat and vegetables. Economical of fuel, as only a small amount of heat is required. Requires little attention during cooking. No loss of nutrients as the liquid is served with the food.
*Disadvantages*: takes a long time.

| HOW | WHY |
|---|---|
| 1. Cut food into small pieces. | To expose maximum surface area to heat. |
| 2. Add sufficient liquid barely to cover food. | To get maximum flavour in the cooking liquid. |
| 3. Make sure the temperature is just below boiling point. | To prevent the food breaking up, meat becoming stringy, and fruit pulping. |
| 4. For a brown stew lightly fry meat and vegetables first. | To improve colour and flavour. |

## Braising

Braising is a method of cookery which combines stewing and baking. It is suitable for medium quality cuts of meat and for vegetables.

The food is cooked until tender in a covered pan with a little fat and a little seasoned liquid. It is then browned in the oven with the lid off.

# 10 Raising agents

*How they work Types of raising agents How they are used*

Raising agents are substances added to flour mixtures in order to make them lighter and more open in texture, and therefore more pleasant to eat and easier to digest. Raising agents are either gases, e.g. air, or substances from which gases are produced, e.g. yeast, baking powder and sodium hydrogen carbonate (bicarbonate of soda). Water acts as a raising agent, it turns to steam on heating.

**How raising agents work**

1. The raising agent provides bubbles of gas in the mixture. Air is incorporated by beating; carbon dioxide is produced by yeast, baking powder or bicarbonate of soda. Bubbles of steam or water vapour are produced from the water when it is heated.
2. These bubbles of gas expand when heated.
3. The protein of flour mixtures, gluten, is elastic and is stretched by the expanding gases.
4. The heat during cooking 'sets' the gluten and so forms the rigid framework of the flour product.

**Types of raising agents**

Air

Air can be introduced into a mixture by:
1. Sieving the flour (the air is trapped between the grains).
2. Raising the flour above the bowl when rubbing in fat.
3. Beating the mixture, as for batters.
4. Creaming fat and sugar as in rich cake making.
5. Whisking eggs (either whole or whites only).
6. Folding between layers as in flaky pastry.

The amount of air included cannot be accurately measured but is judged by the appearance of the mixture, e.g. a whisked sponge mixture should be a thick, stable foam of creamy consistency and colour.

Yeast

Yeast is sometimes known as a biological raising agent, as it is a mass of living micro-organisms which, in the presence of food and moisture, grow and produce carbon dioxide. This reaction takes place more quickly in warm conditions than in cold ones; yeast can be killed by overheating. It can be introduced into a mixture by adding it to the liquid before stirring into the flour, or it can be rubbed into the flour. It is distributed evenly by kneading the dough. If too much yeast is used in bread making, the loaf may have a coarse texture and/or a sour taste. It may also collapse.

The reactions by which yeast breaks down sugar to produce carbon dioxide and alcohol are known as fermentation (see page 104, Principles of yeast cookery).

Chemical raising agents

1. *Bicarbonate of soda used alone*, e.g. in making gingerbread: bicarbonate of soda can be added with the flour. When liquid is incorporated and the mixture is heated, the bicarbonate decomposes and forms carbon dioxide, water and sodium carbonate. The latter substance is alkaline and gives an unpleasant flavour and colour which are masked by ginger and dark treacle.
The chemical reactions when using bicarbonate of soda may be summarized:

$$2\,NaHCO_3 \xrightarrow[\text{moisture}]{\text{heat}} CO_2 + H_2O + Na_2CO_3$$

*sodium hydrogen carbonate* — *carbon dioxide* — *water* — *sodium carbonate*

2. *Bicarbonate of soda used with an acid substance*, e.g. in scones:
a) Used with sour milk – the sodium hydrogen carbonate reacts with lactic acid in the milk forming carbon dioxide, sodium lactate and water.
b) Used with tartaric acid – the reaction is quick and gas may be lost before the mixture is in the oven. Equal quantities of soda and acid are used.
c) Used with cream of tartar, or potassium hydrogen tartrate – the reaction is slow until the dough is heated in the oven when the gas is quickly produced. Use two parts of cream of tartar to one of soda.
(In a) and b) above, the dry acid substances should be sieved with the flour and bicarbonate of soda to mix thoroughly.)
The chemical reactions when using bicarbonate of soda may be summarised:

$$NaHCO_3 + HX \longrightarrow CO_2 + H_2O + NaX$$

*sodium hydrogen carbonate* — *an acid* — *carbon dioxide* — *water* — *a tasteless sodium salt*

3. *Baking-powder:* in the UK commercial baking powder contains bicarbonate of soda mixed with two acid salts, acid calcium phosphate (ACP) and acid sodium pyrophosphate (ASP). Starch is added as a filler and to absorb moisture and thus improve the keeping quality of the powder.

Self-raising flour has baking powder added to it, at the rate of 4 level teaspoons per 400 g flour.

*Note.* When using chemical raising agents doughs are likely to be alkaline and thiamin is completely destroyed during baking, e.g. scones and plain cakes. Yeast mixtures retain their thiamin. The effect of using excessive amounts of a chemical raising agent is that the mixture will rise too rapidly and subsequently sink in the middle. Too much bicarbonate of soda in a mixture gives a sour taste.

Water vapour

Liquids used in mixtures produce water vapour or steam when heated which acts as a raising agent. This is especially important in batters and flaky, puff and choux pastries. The high proportion of water in these recipes produces, when heated, a large volume of water vapour. These mixtures must be cooked in a pre-heated, hot oven.

# 11 Mixtures using flour, and puddings

*Pastry Cakes Batters Biscuits Scones Yeast mixtures Pudding making*

## Pastry making

Pastry is a mixture of flour, salt, fat and water. The variety and texture of the pastry depends on the proportions of these ingredients, on the way in which they are incorporated and on the method of cooking.

Ingredients for pastry making

1. *Flour*: use plain flour, preferably a 'weak' one for shortcrust and suet pastries, and a 'strong' one for flaky and puff pastries.
2. *Baking powder*: use only in suet pastry (or in shortcrust pastry if it is necessary to use less than half fat to flour).
3. *Salt*: use 1 teaspoonful to each 500 g of flour to improve the flavour and to strengthen the gluten.
4. *Water*: use as cold as possible, add just enough to obtain the desired consistency.
5. *Lemon juice*: this may be added to the richer pastries to make the gluten more elastic.
6. *Fat*: use the type and quantity required for the recipe, which will also determine the method of adding the fat. Suet, butter, margarine, cooking fat, lard, or a mixture of margarine and lard or of butter and lard may be used, according to the type of pastry.

Aims in pastry making

1. *Lightness*: depends on the amount of raising agent. In most pastries, this raising agent is air which expands when heated. Baking powder is used in suet pastry, as suet melts slowly and the starch grains in the flour may harden before absorbing the fat. Suet pastry is best cooked by steaming or boiling, as baking hardens it.
2. *Shortness*: short pastry should crumble easily. This is achieved by rubbing in fat without oiling, by using only just enough water to bind it together, by light handling and by baking in a hot oven.

In making shortcrust pastry, fat is wrapped around groups of flour particles making a waterproof layer. Some flour particles remain free and combine with the small amount of added water. This develops just sufficient of the gluten to form a meshwork in the pastry which, on baking, becomes crisp. If too much gluten is developed the pastry may be tough.

3. *Flakiness* (in rough puff, flaky and puff pastries): it is achieved by folding in the maximum amount of air, by careful rolling and by baking at the correct oven temperature. The higher propor-

tion of water in these pastries ensures that sufficient gluten is developed to make thin layers of elastic dough. The flakiness arises from layers of dough separated by layers of fat and air pockets.

**General rules for pastry making**

1. Use good quality plain flour.
2. Keep everything as cool as possible.
3. Introduce as much air as possible during the making.
4. Allow pastries (except suet) to relax after making.
5. Roll lightly with short quick forward strokes.
6. Bake at the correct oven temperature; the richer the pastry, the hotter the oven. (See table on page 94.)

**Principles of pastry making**

1. Air incorporated during making expands during cooking.
2. The expanding air stretches the elastic gluten of the flour.
3. The fat melts.
4. The starch grains in the flour swell and gelatinise in the heat, and absorb the fat and some water.
5. The gluten coagulates and sets the 'framework' of the pastry.
6. Surplus water evaporates.
7. The starch grains on the surface are turned to dextrin in baking, thus giving a brown colour to the pastry.

*Note.* A hot oven must be used, otherwise the fat will melt before the starch gelatinises and the fat will run out.

*The most common types of pastry:*

**Suet pastry**

| HOW | WHY |
|---|---|
| 1. Sieve 250 g flour with 1 rounded teaspoon baking powder and 1 level teaspoon salt. | To aerate the flour. Baking powder to provide extra raising agent. Salt to improve flavour. |
| 2. Add 75 g suet finely chopped, or shredded, and mix. | To distribute it evenly in the mixture, it is too hard to rub in. |
| 3. Add about 125 ml cold water to make a soft but not sticky dough. Knead lightly. | To make a smooth, even dough. Steam from the water acts as a supplementary raising agent. |
| 4. Roll to required shape. | |
| 5. Cook by steaming. | Suet melts slowly – a slow moist method is best. |

**Shortcrust pastry**

| HOW | WHY |
|---|---|
| 1. Sieve 250 g plain flour with 1 level teaspoon salt. | To aerate the flour and to improve the flavour. |
| 2. Add 125 g fat (half butter or margarine, half lard). | Lard gives short texture. Butter and margarine give colour and flavour. |

| | |
|---|---|
| 3. Rub fat into flour with tips of fingers, including as much air as possible. | To keep the mixture as cool as possible and to aerate it. |
| 4. Add about 50 ml very cold water and mix to a stiff dough. | Too much water makes a tough pastry. |
| 5. Knead lightly. | To make an even dough. |
| 6. Set the dough aside in a cool place to relax. | To avoid shrinkage in cooking. |
| 7. Roll once only into shape required. Roll lightly. | To avoid stretching the pastry. |
| 8. Cook in a hot oven. | To cause rapid expansion of air, gelatinisation of the starch grains and absorption of the fat. |

*Alternative all-in-one method:*

| | |
|---|---|
| 1. Place fat, water and ⅓ flour in bowl and cream with fork. | Forms a water-in-fat emulsion stabilised with flour. |
| 2. Stir in remaining flour to form a firm dough. | Flour particles are surrounded by the water-in-fat emulsion which prevents the joining together of the gluten. |
| 3. Knead until smooth and silky. | Gluten does not develop so pastry has short texture. |

## Rough puff pastry

| HOW | WHY |
|---|---|
| 1. Sieve 250 g flour and 1 level teaspoon salt. | To aerate the flour. |
| 2. Cream 150 g fat and cut into about twelve lumps. Use 100 g butter and margarine and 50 g lard. | Fat should be of the same consistency as the dough. |
| 3. Toss the fat in the flour. | To separate the lumps. |
| 4. Add 125 ml cold water and ¼ teaspoon lemon juice to make a soft dough. | Steam from the water acts as a raising agent. Lemon juice makes gluten more elastic. |
| 5. Mix with a palette knife. | To avoid breaking the fat. |
| 6. Shape into a rectangle and roll lightly into a long strip. | |

| | | |
|---|---|---|
| | 7. Fold neatly into three, enclosing as much air as possible. Close and seal ends. | To separate each layer of pastry with air. |
| | 8. Give pastry a half turn and repeat the rolling and folding twice more. | To give several layers to the pastry. |
| | 9. Set it aside to relax. | To avoid shrinkage during cooking. |
| | 10. Roll into shape required. | |
| | 11. Bake in a very hot oven. | To cause rapid expansion of air and to gelatinise the starch grains and so enable them to absorb the fat as it melts. |

*Alternative*: hard margarine from the freezer can be grated into the flour, then continue as from point 3.

| | **HOW** | **WHY** |
|---|---|---|
| Flaky pastry | 1. Sieve 250 g flour and 1 level teaspoon salt. | To aerate the flour. |
| | 2. Cream 175 g of fat. Use 135 g margarine and 40 g lard. | To make the fat the same consistency as the dough. |
| | 3. Rub ¼ of the fat into the flour and mix to a soft dough with 125 ml cold water and ¼ teaspoon lemon juice. | A soft dough is easy to roll and of the same consistency as the fat. |
| | 4. Knead lightly. | To develop gluten.<br>To make a smooth dough. |
| | 5. Roll into an even oblong strip and put another ¼ of the fat in small lumps on to ⅔ of the dough. | To ensure even distribution of the fat. |
| | 6. Fold evenly to produce alternate layers of dough and fat. Seal the edges with the rolling pin. | To enclose as much air as possible and to produce the flaky layers. |
| | 7. Give pastry a half turn and repeat the rolling and addition of fat twice more. | |
| | 8. Allow pastry to relax in a cool place. | To avoid shrinkage during cooking. |
| | 9. Roll and fold twice more. | To make pastry really flaky. |

| | |
|---|---|
| 10. Bake in a very hot oven for 15–20 minutes. | To expand the air and thus to separate the layers. |
| 11. Reduce temperature slightly. | To cook thoroughly. |

*Flaky pastry*

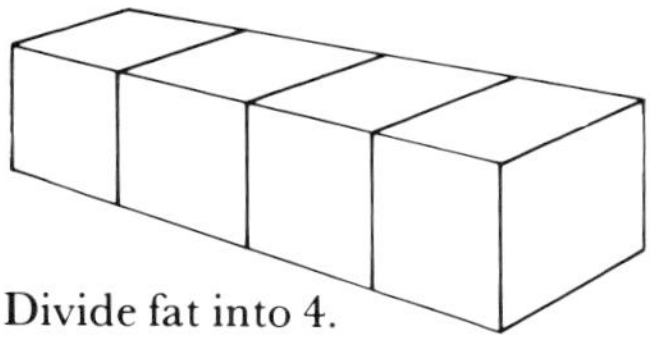

1 Divide fat into 4.

Rub in ¼ fat. Add cold water and lemon juice to make soft dough

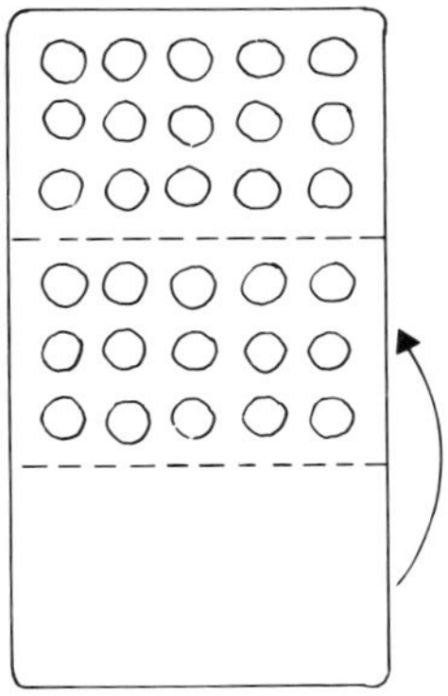

2 Roll dough to a rectangle. Place ¼ fat on ⅔ dough in small pats

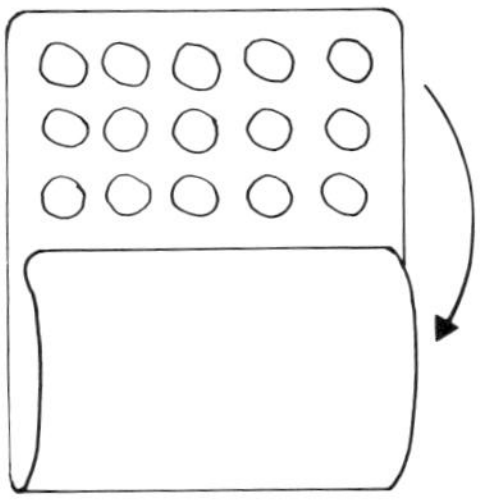

3 Fold up the ⅓ dough with no fat to cover dough with fat. Fold down top ⅓ dough

4 Half turn dough and seal edges with rolling pin.

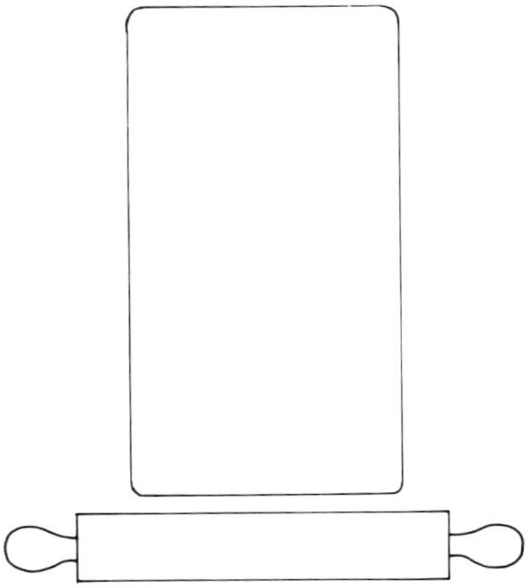

5 Roll to rectangle again and repeat addition of fat twice more.
Rest in cool place

*Alternative method*

1. Make dough without any fat.
2. Knead very well as for bread.
3. Roll out and put ⅓ of the fat on ⅔ of the pastry.

Continue as in previous recipe.

**Table comparing the most common pastries**

| | *Suet* | *Short* | *Rough puff* | *Flaky* |
|---|---|---|---|---|
| Flour | Plain, soft with baking powder, or self-raising flour | Plain, soft | Plain, strong | Plain, strong |
| Type of fat | Suet | ½ butter or margarine plus ½ lard | ⅔ butter or margarine plus ⅓ lard | ¾ butter or margarine plus ¼ lard |
| Proportion of fat to flour | ⅓ | ½ | ⅔ | ¾ |
| Raising agent | Baking powder | Air | Air and water vapour | Air and water vapour |
| Consistency | Soft | Stiff | Soft | Soft |
| Method of cooking | Steaming, boiling or baking in a moderate oven | Baking in a hot oven or frying | Baking in a very hot oven | Baking in a very hot oven |
| Uses | Steamed puddings, dumplings, jam rolypoly | Fruit pies, pasties, tarts, flans, meat pies using pre-cooked meat | Meat pies, sausage rolls, mince pies, Eccles cakes | As for rough puff |

Failures in pastry making

Failures may be due to any of the following reasons:
1. Insufficient air has been incorporated or, in suet pastry, not enough baking powder has been used.
2. Too much liquid, causing a hard and tough pastry.
3. Too much handling in rolling out, causing a hard, badly risen pastry.
4. No time allowed for relaxing of pastry, which then shrinks on cooking.
5. Too cool an oven, causing an ill-risen greasy pastry.
6. Too cool an oven, causing pastry to be hard on the outside and soggy inside.

## Cake making

Ingredients for cake making

Cakes are made from a mixture of flour, sugar and (usually) fat, eggs and a liquid. They vary in taste and texture according to the proportions of the ingredients used, and the method of preparation and of cooking.
1. *Flour*: use a 'weak' or 'soft' flour, i.e. one with a high starch and low gluten content. This gives cakes a fine, even texture. For plain cake mixtures self-raising flour may be used, but for rich mixtures plain flour is better, as the amount of baking powder

needed depends on the type of mixture and the amount of air included.

2. *Sugar*: use caster sugar, unless otherwise specified in the recipe, as it dissolves easily and creams readily with fat. Soft brown sugar may be used in fruit cakes and gingerbread, to give a dark colour. Sugar sweetens the mixture, helps to brown the outside of the cake as it caramelises during baking, and makes the gluten framework soft in texture.

3. *Fat*: butter gives the best flavour but margarine is a good substitute. Both cream easily with sugar. Cooking fats cream easily but have very little flavour. Lard and dripping are inexpensive but have characteristic tastes which, in some mixtures, can be disguised with spices. Fats are used to give a soft texture and a good flavour, and to improve the keeping quality of the mixture.

A plain cake is one with less than half fat to flour. A rich cake is one with half or more fat to flour.

Fat may be added to cake mixtures in one of four methods:

a) Rubbing into the flour with the fingertips.
b) Creaming with the sugar.
c) Melting, usually with sugar or treacle, and adding to the dry ingredients.
d) All-in-one method using soft margarine.

4. *Eggs*: when beaten, eggs have the property of entangling air, which acts as a raising agent. The protein of eggs together with the gluten of the flour forms the framework of the cooked cake. Eggs also give flavour and colour, and the fat in the yolk enriches the mixture.

5. *Liquids*: the liquids used are milk, water or eggs, and the amount depends on the required consistency of the mixture. Milk increases the food value and improves the flavour. Eggs do both these things and also help in the raising. Liquids are necessary to bind the mixture, to make the gluten elastic, to dissolve soluble constituents such as sugar, to enable baking powder to produce carbon dioxide, and to provide steam which helps to raise the cake.

6. *Raising agents*: air is the main raising agent and is added to mixtures by:

a) Rubbing fat into flour.
b) Creaming fat and sugar.
c) Whisking eggs alone or with sugar.

Baking powder is used in plain cake mixtures (or self-raising flour may be used). Bicarbonate of soda is used in gingerbread mixtures as it helps to make them dark in colour, and the spices disguise the taste of the sodium carbonate left in the mixture.

### Aims in cake making

1. Even 'open' texture which depends on the correct proportion of ingredients and on correct mixing and cooking.

2. Good and even rising which depends on the correct amount of raising agent and on correct baking.

3. Attractive appearance, which depends on correct baking.
4. Pleasant flavour, which depends on using good quality ingredients in the correct proportions.

General rules for cake making

1. Prepare the tin: for plain and whisked mixtures grease lightly. For rich and melted fat mixtures line the tin with greaseproof paper.
2. Weigh or measure the ingredients accurately.
3. In mixing:
a) Mix dry ingredients thoroughly, by sieving.
b) Blend fat in carefully.
c) Fold in flour very lightly.
d) Dry any fruit well, before adding to mixture.
e) Mix to the correct consistency according to the recipe.
4. Bake mixture at the correct heat for the particular cake, as given in the recipe. In general:
a) The richer the cake, the slower the oven.
b) The larger the cake, the slower the oven.
5. Test to see if cake is cooked. Cake should be:
a) Springy to the touch.
b) Well risen and brown.
c) Shrinking from the sides of the tin.
6. Cool well on a wire rack, and store in an airtight tin.

Principles of cake making

1. *By the rubbing-in method*: rubbing in evenly distributes the fat in the mixture. When liquid is added, the bicarbonate of soda and acid react to give off carbon dioxide.
2. a) *By the creaming method*: when fat and sugar are creamed together air is incorporated, more air is introduced when the eggs are beaten into the mixture. Flour is later folded in carefully. If flour is beaten in, this will knock the air out of the mixture.
b) By the all-in-one method: all the ingredients are beaten together. Soft margarine mixes readily with the other ingredients and enables air to be incorporated. Some baking powder is added as additional raising agent.
3. *By the whisking method*: whisked egg and sugar entangle air. The flour is again folded in carefully, and not beaten.
4. *By the melted fat method*: melted fat is added with the liquid, since this ensures even distribution. Bicarbonate of soda is the usual raising agent, when heated it gives off carbon dioxide.

Effect of cooking on cakes

*In all cakes the following changes occur*:
When put into the oven the mixture becomes hot, and the gases in the mixture (carbon dioxide and air) and the water vapour produced from the liquids expand, stretching the elastic gluten of the flour, and so making the cake rise. The gluten and the egg

proteins 'set' with the heat of the oven to form the framework of the cake. The heat also causes the starch grains in the flour to gelatinise and the fat to melt. The fat and other liquids are absorbed by the starch grains and some of the water evaporates. On the outside the starch is turned to dextrin and the sugar to caramel, giving the brown colour to the finished cake. The Maillard reaction between protein and sugar also contributes to the brown colour (see page 4).

Failure in cake making

This may be due to:
1. Too much or too little raising agent.
2. Wrong proportion of other ingredients.
3. Too much or too little liquid and therefore wrong consistency.
4. Not whisking or creaming enough or too vigorous beating or folding in of flour.
5. Too hot or too cold an oven.

*Methods of cake making*

Melted fat method – e.g. gingerbread

| **HOW** | **WHY** |
|---|---|
| 1. Sieve 250 g flour with all dry ingredients. | To aerate flour and to mix thoroughly. |
| 2. Heat 75 g fat, 75 g sugar and 100 g syrup. Let fat melt but do not overcook. | To avoid changes in the sugar caused by overheating. |
| Cool. | To prevent cooking of the flour when added. |
| 3. Add mixture to dry ingredients together with enough liquid to make thick batter. | To blend thoroughly and to start action of raising agent. |
| 4. Mix gently with metal spoon but do not beat. | To avoid a tough texture. |
| 5. Pour into a greased and lined tin. | To prevent burning and sticking. |
| 6. Bake in a low oven (150°C, Gas 2) until well risen and firm. | Carbon dioxide is produced slowly from bicarbonate of soda. Cake would burn at higher temperature because of the high sugar content. |
| 7. Keep for 24 hours before eating. | Mixture improves with keeping, centre becomes soft, and the outside sticky. |

| | HOW | WHY |
|---|---|---|
| Rubbing-in method – e.g. economical fruit cake | 1. Sieve 200 g flour, pinch of salt and 1 level teaspoon baking powder. | To aerate the mixture. |
| | 2. Rub 75–100 g fat in with fingertips. | To distribute evenly. |
| | 3. Add 75–100 g sugar, flavourings, and mix with beaten egg and milk to make soft, dropping consistency. | To blend thoroughly and to start action of baking powder. |
| | 4. Put into greased cake tin. | To prevent sticking. |
| | 5. Bake large cake in a moderate oven (180°C, Gas 4) and small cakes in hot oven (200°C, Gas 6). | To allow the carbon dioxide to expand before the gluten sets framework of cake. |
| | 6. Store in an airtight tin but use within three days. | To stop the cakes from going dry because the proportion of fat is low. |

| | HOW | WHY |
|---|---|---|
| Creaming method – e.g. Victoria sandwich | 1. Beat 100 g fat and 100 g sugar with wooden spoon until light and creamy. | To enclose air and to break down sugar crystals. |
| | 2. Beat 2 eggs until light and fluffy. | To enclose air. |
| | 3. Add eggs gradually, beating well. | To prevent 'curdling', i.e. fat separating from sugar and eggs. |
| | 4. Sieve 150 g flour and ½ level teaspoon baking powder and fold in lightly with a metal spoon. | To add more air and to avoid knocking air out by beating in flour. |
| | 5. Put into a paper-lined tin. Greasing is not usually necessary. | To prevent burning. There is usually enough fat in mixture to prevent sticking. |
| | 6. Bake in a moderate oven (190°C, Gas 5) for small cakes (170°C, Gas 3) for large cakes. | To allow gases to expand before gluten sets. |
| | 7. Cool when cooked and store in airtight tin where the cakes can be kept for some time. | Because the high fat content keeps them moist. |

*Alternative all-in-one method:*

| HOW | WHY |
|---|---|
| 1. Put the same ingredients in the mixing bowl all together. Use a soft margarine, roughly cut, and unbeaten eggs. | This saves time in preparation. |
| 2. Add 2 tablespoonfuls of milk and an extra, level teaspoon of baking powder. | The extra liquid makes the mixture easier to beat, and the extra raising agent replaces the air incorporated by the ordinary methods. |
| 3. Beat for 1 minute with a wooden spoon. | |
| 4. Bake as usual. | |

Whisking method – e.g. Swiss roll

| HOW | WHY |
|---|---|
| 1. Whisk 2 eggs and 50 g sugar together until thick and creamy. (This will be easier over a pan of hot water.) | Sugar dissolves and air is held by the mixture. Warming allows more air to be incorporated. |
| Continue whisking off the heat for 2 minutes. | To make a thick, stable foam. |
| 2. Sieve 50 g flour and a pinch of baking powder evenly over the mixture. | To separate the flour grains. |
| 3. Fold flour in carefully with a metal spoon. | To avoid knocking out air. |
| 4. Pour into tins, greased and sprinkled with caster sugar and flour. | This gives a sweet crusty outside to the cake. |
| 5. Bake immediately in a moderate oven (180°C, Gas 4) until set. Do not open oven door too soon. | Mixture easily sinks if cooled by air before it is set. |
| 6. Turn out on to a wire rack and cool away from draughts. | To ensure even cooling. |
| 7. Do not store long before use. | As they contain no fat, they dry quickly. |

(The above is sometimes called a fatless sponge mixture.)

**Table comparing methods of cake making**

| | *Melted fat method* | *Rubbing-in method* | *Creaming method* | *Whisking method* |
|---|---|---|---|---|
| Proportion of ingredients | ⅓ fat to flour<br>⅓ sugar to flour | ⅓–½ fat to flour<br>⅓–½ sugar to flour | ½–1 fat to flour<br>½–1 sugar to flour | No fat<br>50 g sugar 50 g flour to every egg used |
| | ⅔ treacle or syrup to flour<br>1 egg to 250 g flour (optional) | 1 egg to 200g flour | 2–4 eggs to 200 g flour | |
| | Enough milk to make thick batter | Enough milk to make soft dropping consistency | Enough milk to make dropping consistency | Usually no extra milk. Mixture should be thick and creamy |
| Flour and raising agent | S. R. flour + ½ level teaspoon bicarbonate of soda to 250 g flour | S.R. flour or plain flour + 2 level teaspoons baking powder to 200 g flour | Plain flour with amount of baking powder decreasing with richness | Plain or S.R. flour |
| Fat and method of adding it | Lard, margarine or dripping melted with sugar and syrup, and added to dry ingredients | Margarine or butter rubbed into flour with fingertips | Margarine or butter beaten with sugar until creamy | None |
| Oven heats | | | | |
| Large cakes: | 150°C, Gas 2 | 180°C, Gas 4 | 170°C, Gas 3 | 180°C, Gas 4 |
| Small cakes: | 180°C, Gas 4 | 200°C, Gas 6 | 190°C, Gas 5 | 180°C, Gas 4 |
| Examples | | | | |
| Large cakes: | Gingerbread | Plain fruit cake | Victoria sandwich | Sponge sandwich |
| | Malt loaf | Coconut cake | Christmas cake | Swiss roll |
| Small cakes: | Gingerbuns | Rock cakes | Queen cakes | Sponge cakes |
| | Parkins | Jam buns | Cup cakes | Sponge fingers |

## Batter making

Batters are mixtures of flour, milk and sometimes eggs. Strong flour gives the best results as the gluten gives a good elastic structure. Batter rises during cooking because air incorporated during mixing expands. Also water vapour formed from the liquid used enlarges these air pockets and is an important part of the raising action. The effect of egg is to help retain the air beaten into the mixture until the batter is set by cooking. If no eggs are used additional raising agent may be needed such as baking powder or yeast.

Types of batters

1. *Plain coating batter*: used for coating foods before frying. 100 g flour is blended with 125 ml milk, and salt and baking powder or yeast added. This forms a thick coating batter.
2. *Egg batter*: 100 g plain flour is blended with 1 egg and 250 ml milk and whisked to incorporate air. This makes a thin batter for pancakes, Yorkshire puddings, toad-in-the-hole, batter puddings, etc.

Aims in batter making

1. Lightness. This depends on
a) The amount of gluten and egg in the mixture which affects the amount of 'rise' obtained.
b) The correct cooking temperature, i.e. high at first to cause rapid expansion of the gases and, later, a lower temperature to ensure that the inside is cooked.
2. Crispness in baked or fried batters. This depends on the correct temperature of the oven or of frying fat (190°C, Gas 5). This will brown the outside and also cook the inside thoroughly without burning.

Principles of making batter

1. Air is beaten into the mixture. Egg albumen retains air.
2. Water vaporises in heat of cooking.
3. Gases and water vapour expand on heating and stretch the elastic gluten in the mixture.
4. Albumen of egg and gluten of flour set in the heat.
5. Starch grains gelatinise in the heat and absorb liquid.
6. Starch on the outside is turned to dextrin. Maillard reaction also contributes brown colour.

Basic egg batter

| HOW | WHY |
|---|---|
| 1. Sieve 100 g plain, strong flour and 1 level teaspoon salt. | To mix and aerate. Salt adds flavour. |
| 2. Make a hollow in centre of flour, add 1 egg. Stir well. | To blend ingredients smoothly. |
| 3. Add 125 ml milk to make a creamy consistency. Beat or whisk thoroughly. | To incorporate as much air as possible and remove all lumps of dry flour. |
| 4. Add a further 125 ml of milk. Stir. | Difficult to beat if batter is very liquid. |
| 5. *Baking*: Pour into hot well-greased tin. Bake in hot oven (200°C, Gas 6). *Frying*: Fry in hot fat. | To obtain a well risen and thoroughly cooked batter. |

## Biscuits

Biscuits may be made by any of the methods of cake making, but they differ from cakes in:
1. *Consistency of mixture*: this is usually very stiff, so little or no liquid is used.

2. *Aeration*: the texture required is crisp, so little or no raising agent is used.
3. *Shape and size*: after kneading, the mixture is rolled and cut, or piped into required shape.
4. *Baking temperature*: they are cooked very slowly, so that water is driven off, leaving the biscuits crisp and dry.

Aims in biscuit making

1. *A short crisp texture*: this can be obtained by using a soft flour, or a mixture of cornflour and wheat flour, by slow baking, and by storing in an airtight tin.
2. *Regular shape*: roll or cut carefully, and have mixture very stiff.
3. *A good colour*: they should be very pale brown. This is obtained by very slow baking.
4. *A pleasant flavour*: use good quality ingredients in the correct proportions.

Methods of biscuit making

1. By melted fat method, e.g. ginger nuts, parkin biscuits, brandy snaps and flapjacks.
2. By rubbing-in method e.g. shortbread, oatmeal, cheese and coconut biscuits.
3. By creaming method, e.g. Shrewsbury and Easter biscuits, and some shortbread.
4. By the whisking method, e.g. sponge fingers and sponge drops.

**Scones**

Types of scones

1. Oven scones may be plain, sweet (with fruit, sugar or syrup) or savoury (with cheese). They may be made with white or brown flour or a mixture of flour and oatmeal.
2. Girdle scones may be made with a similar mixture.
3. Drop scones may be made from a thick egg batter, and are cooked on a hot girdle or hotplate.

All scone mixtures are plain, i.e. they contain only a small proportion of fat and sugar (see Cake making). Except for the batter scones, the method of making is the rubbing-in method. The raising agent may be:

a) baking powder *or*
b) bicarbonate of soda and cream of tartar *or*
c) bicarbonate of soda and sour milk.

The mixture should be light and soft in texture, and cooked at a high temperature (200–230°C, Gas 6–8) so that the gases expand quickly and the dough sets quickly. They do not burn easily as they contain little fat or sugar and, for the same reason, they get dry quickly after cooking and should therefore be eaten the same day.

The old slogan for scones was: 'very cold making, very hot baking'.

## Yeast mixtures

Yeast mixtures are doughs of flour, salt, sugar and a liquid, which are caused to rise by the action of yeast. Rich yeast mixtures may also contain fat, eggs, extra sugar and fruit. The liquid is usually water, milk or a mixture of both.

Ingredients for yeast cookery

1. *Flour*: use a 'hard' or 'strong' flour, i.e. one with a relatively high gluten content. This makes an elastic dough when mixed with water and kneaded. Use plain flour, as no chemical raising agent is needed. If wholemeal flour is used, more liquid will be required as the bran absorbs water.
2. *Salt*: provides flavour, helps to make a firm gluten framework and controls the action of yeast.
3. *Yeast*: consists of masses of living organisms. These can be mixed with a starchy material and then either dried sufficiently to be compressed into cakes (compressed yeast), or more thoroughly dried (dried yeast) when it will keep wholesome for several months. The dried yeast must be soaked in tepid water before use. Compressed yeast looks like putty; if fresh it should be fawn in colour, crumble easily and have a pleasant characteristic smell. It will keep fresh for about a week if wrapped and stored in the refrigerator, or if kept in a basin of cold water.
4. *Sugar*: provides food for the yeast so that it can grow and begin its work in the dough. The yeast ferments the sugar and produces carbon dioxide. Too much sugar retards the action of the yeast.
5. *Liquids*: water is needed to develop the gluten into an elastic framework, to dissolve sugar and salt in the mixture, and to enable the yeast to work. Milk may be used instead of water. This improves the flavour of the dough and increases its food value.
6. *Fat*: is sometimes added to enrich doughs and to improve their keeping qualities. Butter, lard or margarine may be used.
7. *Eggs*: may be added to enrich the dough.

Aims in yeast cookery

1. *Good appearance*: loaves, rolls and buns should be regular in shape with an evenly browned outside. This is achieved by skill in shaping and care in baking. Strong flour produces a loaf of good volume.
2. *Even rising*: depends on correct treatment of the yeast, good kneading and careful cooking.
3. *Open and springy texture*: can be obtained by adding the correct amount of water to produce a springy, not tight dough, by allowing the yeast to work sufficiently but not to 'overprove', and by placing the dough in a hot oven.
4. *Good flavour*: depends on the correct proportion of salt and other good quality ingredients. Variety can be obtained by using wholemeal or germ meal flour, or by mixing white flour with rye flour.

*Short-time doughs*
The traditional method of bread making involves many stages which take time. At research laboratories at Chorleywood, a new method has been developed which reduces the time.

Ascorbic acid acts as a flour improver; it accelerates the reactions which develop the gluten into an elastic meshwork in the dough. The initial rising period is replaced by intensive kneading and a short rest of 5–10 minutes.

The basic recipe is similar, with the following variations:
1. Household plain flour may be used instead of strong flour.
2. Ascorbic acid is dissolved in the liquid, approx. 25 mg per 500 g flour. (Tablets of 50 mg ascorbic acid may be bought from the chemist.)
3. A small amount of fat is necessary, about 25 g per 500 g flour.
4. Fresh yeast gives a better flavour than dried yeast.

Principles of yeast cookery

1. Yeast consists of a mass of single-celled living organisms which, when given food and moisture, grow by 'budding'. While growing, yeast produces enzymes which act on sugars to split them up into simpler substances. This action, known as *fermentation*, takes place more quickly in warm conditions. In bread making this occurs as follows:
a) The warm, moist conditions in the dough activate the enzyme amylase (diastase) of the wheat flour. The amylase changes some of the starch in the flour into the disaccharide maltose.
b) Yeast produces the enzyme maltase which turns this maltose into the simple sugar glucose.
c) Yeast produces the enzyme sucrase which turns the added sugar sucrose into glucose and fructose.
d) Yeast produces a mixture of enzymes, known as zymase, which change glucose into carbon dioxide and alcohol. It is the carbon dioxide thus produced which is of chief importance in bread making. Like all gases the carbon dioxide expands when heated and so causes the dough to rise. Air, introduced during kneading, is necessary for the production of carbon dioxide, in the absence of oxygen more alcohol is produced.

Summary of the changes:

| | | |
|---|---|---|
| Starch | $\xrightarrow{\textit{flour amylase}}$ | maltose |
| Maltose | $\xrightarrow{\textit{yeast maltase}}$ | glucose |
| Sucrose | $\xrightarrow{\textit{yeast sucrase}}$ | glucose and fructose |
| Glucose | $\xrightarrow{\textit{yeast zymase}}$ | carbon dioxide and alcohol |

2. The flour proteins absorb the added liquid and form an elastic complex called gluten. When the dough is kneaded and risen, the gluten develops into a meshwork which traps the bubbles of carbon dioxide formed by the yeast. The gluten is elastic and stretches as the carbon dioxide is produced, so causing the dough to rise. The time taken for the dough to rise depends on temperature, the stiffness of the dough and the amount of yeast and sugar present. The time is considerably reduced if ascorbic acid is present, as in the short-time method.

3. The heat used in cooking the bread has the following effects:
a) The yeast is killed and the enzymes inactivated.
b) The bubbles of carbon dioxide, water vapour and air throughout the dough expand and stretch the gluten. This rise in the dough is called oven-spring.
c) The starch grains absorb water, swell and gelatinise.
d) The gluten coagulates or 'sets'.
e) The water and alcohol evaporate.
f) The crust is formed by starch turning to dextrins, sugar caramelising and gluten becoming brown and crisp.

Bread making

| **HOW** | **WHY** |
|---|---|
| 1. Sieve 500 g flour and 2 level teaspoons salt into warm bowl and stand in a warm place. | Sieve to aerate and remove lumps. Add salt to give flavour and give firmness to gluten. Keep warm to help yeast to work. |
| 2. Disperse 15 g yeast and 1 teaspoon sugar in 250 ml liquid warmed to 27°C. | Yeast is well distributed when added with the liquid. Yeast produces enzymes which begin to act on sugar. |
| 3. Add the liquid all at once to the flour. | To make a soft dough which leaves the sides of the bowl clean. |
| 4. Knead the dough until the texture is smooth. | To develop the meshwork of gluten, and to distribute the yeast. |
| 5. Put the dough in a covered bowl or plastic bag to rise until twice the size. | Cover to prevent skinning or drying. Time needed for yeast to produce carbon dioxide which stretches the gluten. |
| 6. Knead lightly and shape into loaves or rolls. | To introduce air and remove large bubbles of gas. |
| 7. Put to rise again (about 10 minutes) in a warm place. | To allow further fermentation. |
| 8. Bake in a hot oven (230°C, Gas 8). | To kill yeast, inactivate enzymes, expand the gases in the dough. |
| 9. Reduce heat after 10 minutes. | To allow time to set the gluten throughout the loaf, to gelatinise the starch and form the crust. |
| 10. Test for readiness by tapping on bottom of loaf. It should sound hollow. | Gluten framework is set throughout. |
| 11. Allow to cool out of tin. | To allow moisture to evaporate. |

A richer dough for buns and doughnuts etc., may be made by the same method, but the addition of fats and eggs slows down fermentation. For this reason, the proportion of yeast is sometimes increased or a preliminary 'sponging' is done. The yeast is dispersed in the liquid and made into a batter with some of the flour and sugar. When fermentation has begun, the spongy or frothy batter is then mixed with the rest of the flour, fat and sugar.

**Pudding making**

A pudding or a sweet usually forms a separate course in a meal, and is eaten after the main protein dish. It may provide useful amounts of energy foods in the form of sugar and starch, as well as protein, fats, vitamins and mineral salts.

Types of puddings

1. *Flour mixtures* made by any of the pastry or cake making methods:
a) Suet mixtures, e.g. spotted dog, Christmas pudding.
b) Suet pastry puddings, e.g. jam roll, boiled fruit pudding.
c) Baked pastry puddings, e.g. flans, pies, tarts.
d) Cake mixture puddings, e.g. canary pudding.
e) Batters, e.g. pancakes, fritters, fruit in batter.

2. *Milk puddings* made of a cereal cooked in milk with sugar and flavouring added, or just made of milk set with rennet (junket).
a) *Milk cereal puddings*. Usually 35 g cereal to 500 ml milk.
  i) Whole grain, e.g. rice.
  ii) Ground grain, e.g. semolina, ground rice.
  iii) Powdered grain, e.g. cornflour, custard powder.
Milk cereal puddings may be served hot, or made into moulds by increasing the amount of cereal, 50 g to 500 ml milk, and served cold. During cooking the starch grains in the cereal swell, gelatinise and absorb the milk. These puddings may be enriched by the addition of eggs.

Tapioca and sago are not cereals but starchy substances used in a similar way to thicken milk puddings.

b) *Junkets*: these are made by adding rennet and a flavouring to lukewarm milk (at 35°C). Rennet contains the enzyme rennin which coagulates the milk protein caseinogen. Do not overheat or the rennin is inactivated. Keep in a warm place until the junket is set to allow the enzyme to work.

3. *Egg puddings* in which egg is the chief ingredient.
a) Sweet omelettes, in which the beaten eggs are cooked in hot butter.
b) Custards, in which eggs are cooked with milk.
c) Soufflés, in which egg yolks are added to a panada (a thick white sauce – see page 115) and the stiffly beaten whites are folded in before cooking.

The egg proteins in all egg puddings coagulate with the heat. Over-cooking leads to 'curdling' and must be avoided.

4. *Fruit puddings* may be made with fresh or dried fruit.
a) Fruit may be served raw, stewed or baked.
b) Fruit may be made into moulds, snows, jellies, fools etc. Cooking softens the cellulose in fruit and sieving removes the coarse fibres, making it easier to eat.

5. *Gelatine puddings*, e.g. jellies, creams, cold soufflés. Gelatine is used in the proportion of 10–20 g to 500 ml of milk, fruit juice or purée, cream, custard or a mixture of these. Gelatine is made from the connective tissue of animals but it is a protein of low biological value. It is sold in powder or in 'leaf' form. It dissolves in hot water and on cooling it sets to a jelly.

6. *Ice-creams* are usually frozen mixtures of custard and cream or fruit purée. Many flavours and textures may be obtained. The mixture may be frozen in a domestic freezer or in a special ice-cream freezer.

7. *Instant puddings*: pre-cooked starches are available which can be mixed with flavourings, emulsifiers and stabilisers to produce a dry mix. The powder is whisked into a measured amount of milk to make smooth, creamy, cold puddings.

# 12 Stocks and soups

*How to make stock   Types of soups   General rules for making soups*

## Stock

Stock is liquid obtained from bones, meat, vegetables, or fish by long slow simmering, or more quickly by using a pressure cooker. It gives flavour to dishes such as soups, gravies and *réchauffé* dishes. Although it contains relatively little food value, it does add minerals, vitamins of B complex and a little protein which would otherwise be wasted.

*How to make stock:*

Stock

| HOW | WHY |
|---|---|
| 1. Choose a strong deep pan with a well-fitting lid. | Food must be covered with liquid, and very little evaporation should take place. |
| 2. Cut meat into small pieces. Use cooked or uncooked meat, gristle or skin, broken bones, poultry giblets, bacon rinds. | To expose maximum surface area. |
| Avoid including too much fat. | To prevent stock being greasy. |
| Cut vegetables in large pieces. | To prevent vegetables breaking easily and thus making stock cloudy. |
| 3. Add seasoning and a bunch of herbs. | To improve flavour. |
| 4. Cover with water or liquor from cooking vegetables or meat. | |
| 5. Bring to boil, remove scum. | To prevent stock being cloudy. |
| 6. Simmer for about 2 hours. | To extract all soluble nutrients. |
| 7. Strain and cool. | Solid ingredients are of no further use. |
| 8. Remove fat from top. | Stock should not be greasy. |
| 9. Keep in a refrigerator or a cool place, and boil for 5 minutes daily. It may be frozen. | To prevent stock from going bad. It is a good medium for the growth of bacteria. |

*Note.* Avoid starchy vegetables as these easily go sour. Avoid very strongly flavoured or very salt liquor (e.g. from salt ham) as this gives too strong a flavour to the stock.

Types of stock

1. Meat or bone stock.
2. Vegetable stock for vegetarian dishes.
3. Fish stock for sauces.
4. A quick and simple substitute for stock is a commercial stock cube dissolved in water, which gives flavour but little nourishment. It contains salt so little further seasoning is needed.

**Soups**

Value of soups

1. They act as appetizers by increasing the flow of saliva and gastric juice.
2. They can supply protein, fat or carbohydrate depending on the ingredients used.
3. They can be used to add a hot dish to an otherwise cold meal.
4. They are useful to the cook who wishes to use up small amounts of left-over foods.

How to make soup

1. Follow the recipe carefully, using correct amounts of the main ingredients.
2. Use stock in preference to water.
3. Season and taste carefully.
4. Make soup of the correct consistency. A purée or cream soup should be smooth and free from lumps; a broth should have the meat and vegetables in small pieces.
5. Remove all fat.
6. Serve very hot (or alternatively very cold) with the correct garnish.

Types of soup

1. *Clear meat soups or consommés* (these may contain small pieces of vegetable), e.g. Consommé Julienne, or cold, jellied consommé.
2. *Broths* which contain small pieces of meat, vegetables and cereals, e.g. Scotch broth.
3. *Purées* which are vegetable soups, sieved and usually thick owing to the ingredients used, e.g. lentil soup.
4. *Cream soups* which are made by blending thin vegetable purée with a white roux, e.g. cream of celery soup.
5. *Thickened meat soups* which are strained and then thickened with flour or cornflour at the end of cooking, e.g. oxtail soup.

Consommés and broths

| HOW | WHY |
|---|---|
| 1. Cut meat into small pieces, removing fat and skin. | To expose maximum surface area. |
| 2. Put into pan with cold stock, bring slowly to boil, season. | To extract full flavour from meat. |

| | | |
|---|---|---|
| | 3. Prepare, wash and cut small pieces of vegetables. Add to soup. For broths, add rice or pearl barley. | For extra flavour. |
| | 4. Simmer gently. | To cook contents. |
| | 5. When making consommés, strain off solid particles. | Consommé should be clear. |
| | 6. Taste the soup before serving. | Seasoning can be adjusted. |
| | 7. Garnish with chopped parsley. | To improve appearance. |
| | 8. Serve very hot. | |

| | **HOW** | **WHY** |
|---|---|---|
| Vegetable purées and creams | 1. Prepare vegetables and cut into small pieces. | To enable flavour to be extracted. |
| | 2. Sauté vegetables in melted fat. | To develop flavour and improve food value. |
| | 3. Add cold stock, bring to boil, add seasoning and taste the soup. | |
| | 4. Simmer until vegetables are cooked. | |
| | 5. Sieve, put through a vegetable mill or blender. | To give a smooth consistency. |
| | 6. *For a purée*: thicken, if necessary, with a little blended cornflour. | |
| | Boil well. | To cook cornflour. |
| | Serve very hot with croutons. | |
| | *For a cream soup*: blend with a white roux sauce. | To give extra food value and richer texture. |

| | **HOW** | **WHY** |
|---|---|---|
| Thickened meat soups | 1. Prepare meat and vegetables and cut into small, even-sized pieces. | To ensure extraction of flavour and even cooking. |
| | 2. Fry until golden brown. | To give colour and flavour. |
| | 3. Add stock and seasoning. | |

| | |
|---|---|
| 4. Bring to boil, simmer until tender. | To cook ingredients. |
| 5. Strain solids from the liquid. | Flavour should be in the liquid. |
| 6. Add blended flour and boil well. | To give a smooth texture. |
| 7. Taste the soup.<br>Serve very hot. Garnish with a few small pieces of meat. | Seasoning can be adjusted. |

# 13 Beverages

A beverage is the name given to any drink which supplies the body with the water necessary to maintain health.

Why we need beverages

1. To supply water necessary to eliminate body waste and for carrying out the complex chemical processes of metabolism. (See Chapter 2.)
2. To refresh us, and to quench the thirst which is an indication of the body's need for water.
3. To supply nourishment:
a) Milk drinks supply animal proteins, fats, minerals and vitamins.
b) Fruit juices, if fresh and properly prepared, contain vitamin C.
c) Drinks sweetened with sugar, glucose or lactose supply carbohydrates.
4. To act as stimulants, e.g. tea and coffee contain caffeine, and cocoa contains theobromine; these have a mild stimulating effect on the nervous system.
5. To improve the flow of gastric juices, e.g. meat extracts such as Bovril and Oxo, or yeast extracts such as Marmite, stimulate the appetite because of the extractives they contain. Some also supply all the B complex vitamins.
6. To give an immediate sense of warmth and comfort when the body is cold.

Types of beverage

1. *Tea*: obtained from the leaves of a shrub grown mainly in India, China and Sri Lanka. The leaves are picked, crushed and dried. In this state they are known as green tea. They may then be moistened and allowed to ferment before re-drying. This produces the common black tea. Tea has very little food value, but supplies caffeine which is a nerve stimulant, tannin which is an astringent and can give a bitter flavour, and the essential oils which give tea its aroma. The addition of milk and sugar will significantly increase the energy content.

2. *Coffee*: obtained from the fruit of a shrub grown in South America, East Africa and elsewhere. Each fruit contains two seeds or beans. These are removed from the husk, roasted and ground. Coffee contains more caffeine and tannin than tea, and essential oils which give the flavour. Ground coffee, exposed to

the air, soon loses the essential oils, and therefore its flavour. 'Instant coffee' is produced by the dehydration of liquid coffee.

3. *Cocoa*: obtained from the seeds of a small evergreen tree grown in South America and in West Africa. The seeds (or 'nibs') contain fat which is removed and used as cocoa butter. The rest is ground into a fine powder. Cocoa has more food value than either tea or coffee. It contains fat, starch and small amounts of protein, vitamins and iron as well as the stimulant theobromine. It is made with milk which also supplies nutrients.

4. *Fruit drinks*, e.g. fresh lemon or orange juice. These are chiefly of value for their vitamin C content, and for their refreshing taste. Care must be taken not to boil the juice because this would destroy the vitamin C.

5. *Alcoholic drinks*: made by the fermentation of the maltose in malted grains or of the glucose in fruit juices into carbon dioxide and alcohol. Alcohol has a sedative effect on the central nervous system and this action may seriously affect one's judgement and self-control. The amount of alcohol varies with the type of drink.
a) Beers, stouts and ales contain 5–10 per cent of alcohol, and are made from malted barley.
b) Wines such as sherry, claret and port contain 10–20 per cent alcohol and are made from grape juice.
c) Spirits, such as gin, whisky and brandy, contain about 40 per cent alcohol and are made from liquids fermented and then distilled to increase their alcoholic content.
d) Liqueurs are sweetened and flavoured spirits.

6. *Mineral waters*: some are naturally produced from springs in the earth and are bottled at source, e.g. Vichy water. They contain dissolved mineral salts and carbon dioxide. Others are synthetic products made by charging sweetened and flavoured water with carbon dioxide under pressure, thus making it fizzy. Sweetened drinks of this type may be a considerable source of energy in some diets, so contributing to obesity.

*To make household beverages*:

| **HOW** | **WHY** | |
|---|---|---|
| a) Warm the pot and put in ½–1 teaspoon of tea for each person, i.e. to each 250 ml water. | Amount used depends upon personal taste. | Tea |
| b) Pour on actually boiling water and allow to stand 2–3 minutes. | To extract caffeine and essential oils. | |
| c) Serve at once. | To avoid extracting tannin. | |
| d) Add milk, sugar or lemon as desired. | | |

| | HOW | WHY |
|---|---|---|
| Coffee | a) Warm pot or jug and put in 1 tablespoonful of ground coffee for each 250 ml of water. | |
| | b) Pour on boiling water and stir well. | To mix well. |
| | c) Leave to infuse in a warm place for 8 minutes. | To extract flavour and caffeine. |
| | d) Strain through a fine wire strainer. | To remove grounds. |
| | e) Serve black or with hot milk, or cream and sugar as desired. | |

| | HOW | WHY |
|---|---|---|
| Cocoa | a) Mix cocoa (1 rounded teaspoon for each 250 ml) with a little cold liquid, and sugar to taste. | To blend starchy powder to a smooth paste. |
| | b) Boil remaining milk and/or water and pour on to blended cocoa. | To make a smooth mixture. |
| | c) Return to pan and boil. | To cook starch and to develop flavour. |

| | HOW | WHY |
|---|---|---|
| Fruit juice | a) Peel or grate rind (zest) of fruit thinly and place in pan with sugar and water. | Flavour is mostly in the zest, and pith is often bitter. |
| | b) Boil gently for 5 minutes. | To extract the flavour. |
| | c) Allow to cool, then strain. | To remove peel. |
| | d) Squeeze juice from fruit and add to cold liquid. | Heat destroys vitamin C. |

# 14 Sauces, gravies, seasonings, accompaniments

**Sauces**
Sauces are well flavoured liquids used in cooking or served as accompaniments to dishes. They are often thickened and may be sweet or savoury.

Use of sauces

1. To add flavour to otherwise insipid foods, e.g. cheese sauce with macaroni.
2. To add colour to pale foods, e.g. tomato sauce with white fish.
3. To improve the food value of a dish, e.g. mayonnaise with egg salad.
4. To counteract the richness of certain foods, e.g. apple sauce with pork.
5. To moisten dry foods, e.g. custard sauce with steamed puddings.
6. To bind foods together, e.g. a panada base for croquettes.

Types of sauces

1. Savoury white sauces made with flour, fat and milk, e.g. white sauce, or with the addition of flavourings, stock, eggs or cream.
2. Brown sauces made with flour, fat and stock, e.g. gravy.
3. Blended sauces made with cornflour, custard powder or arrowroot, e.g. custard.
4. Cooked egg sauces, e.g. egg custard.
5. Emulsified sauces using egg, e.g. mayonnaise.
6. Miscellaneous sauces, e.g. fruit sauce, mint sauce, bread sauce.

*Savoury white sauce*
This may be either a plain white sauce or a more elaborate flavoured sauce. The purpose of the sauce and the consistency required determine the quantities of ingredients used.

A pouring sauce should just glaze the back of a wooden spoon and pour easily.

A panada should form a firm paste and just leave the sides of the pan clean.

A coating sauce must coat the back of a wooden spoon and just settle to its own level in the pan.

Quantities of ingredients:

| | *Pouring* | *Coating* | *Panada* |
|---|---|---|---|
| Fat | 15 g | 25 g | 50 g |
| Flour | 15 g | 25 g | 50 g |
| Liquid | 250 ml | 250 ml | 250 ml |

White sauces may be made either by the classic, roux method or by a quick all-in-one method.

**White sauce (by the roux method)**

| HOW | WHY |
|---|---|
| 1. Melt fat in pan, add flour, stir and cook gently until it 'honeycombs'. Stir continuously with a wooden spoon. | Starch grains in flour swell on heating and absorb fat so that lumping is avoided. |
| Do not brown. | Browning spoils appearance of a white sauce. |
| 2. Remove from heat, and add liquid gradually, stirring all the time. | Sauce should be smooth and free from lumps. |
| 3. Return to heat and bring to the boil, stirring all the time. | Starch grains gelatinise and absorb liquid thus thickening sauce. |
| 4. Boil for 4–5 minutes. | To cook starch thoroughly and so to avoid 'raw' taste. |
| *Alternative all-in-one method*: | |
| 1. Place flour in saucepan, add some cold milk and whisk or stir with wooden spoon. | To disperse the flour and remove all lumps. |
| 2. Add rest of milk and the fat and bring to the boil, stirring continuously, over a moderate heat. | Stirring will prevent lumping as the sauce thickens and give a good glossy appearance. |
| 3. Boil 4–5 minutes, add seasoning. | To gelatinise all the starch. |

*Note.* If lumps form in a sauce, remove from heat immediately and beat with a wire whisk until lumps are dispersed. Bring back to the boil.

**Brown sauce (by the roux method)**

Use 15 g flour, 15 g fat and 300 ml vegetable or meat stock.

| HOW | WHY |
|---|---|
| 1. Heat the dripping or lard in a thick pan, add flour. Stir and cook until mixture is golden brown in colour. (This is the brown roux.) | Starch grains swell and absorb fat. Some starch is turned to dextrin, giving the required brown colour. |
| 2. Add cold stock slowly, stirring well. As temperature of the roux is above 100°C add liquid with care. | When stock is added, it does not thicken too quickly and form lumps. Stirring makes sauce smooth and glossy. |

| | |
|---|---|
| 3. Bring to boil and cook for 5 minutes. | To develop flavour and to cook thoroughly to gelatinise the starch. |
| 4. Season, serve hot as gravy, or use for meat dishes. | |

*More elaborate types of roux sauces*:

Flavourings can be introduced by infusing vegetables in the milk, e.g. Béchamel, or by frying vegetables with the roux, e.g. Espagnole. Stock or a mixture of stock and milk is used in a velouté sauce, this may be enriched with cream and egg yolk. Egg and cream are added to the cooked sauce and the sauce must not boil after they have been added. Egg proteins will coagulate on boiling and give a curdled appearance.

Blended sauces – e.g. custard

Blended sauces are thickened with a starchy material, e.g. cornflour, custard powder. For a pouring sauce, use 15 g ground cereal to 300 ml liquid.

| **HOW** | **WHY** |
|---|---|
| 1. Blend powder with a little cold liquid. | To keep grains apart. |
| 2. Boil rest of liquid and pour over blended powder stirring well. | To disperse the swelling starch grains and prevent lumping. |
| 3. Return to heat, and boil for 4 to 5 minutes stirring all the time. | To gelatinise all the starch to avoid a raw taste. |
| 4. Add seasoning, or sugar and flavouring. | |

*Fruit Glaze*

Arrowroot is a starchy powder which can be used to make a clear glaze for use on a fruit gateau or flan. 1 teaspoonful of arrowroot is used to thicken 125 ml of syrup from canned fruit, and the method for blended sauces is used. The glaze must be brushed or poured over the fruit while it is still hot to give a smooth finish.

Cooked egg sauces

For egg custard, use 1 egg to 175 ml milk and 25 g sugar.

| **HOW** | **WHY** |
|---|---|
| 1. Beat egg and sugar lightly. | Sufficient to mix yolk and white but not enough to incorporate air. |
| 2. Heat milk to approx. blood temperature and pour on to beaten mixture, stirring well. | |

| | |
|---|---|
| 3. Heat gently, preferably in a double pan or over a low heat, stirring well until sauce thickens slightly. Do not boil. | Gentle heating causes even coagulation of egg proteins and even thickening of sauce. Boiling causes curdling. |

Emulsified sauces

For mayonnaise, use 1 egg yolk to about 125 ml oil.

| HOW | WHY |
|---|---|
| 1. Mix yolk with seasoning. | Mustard and egg lecithin act as emulsifiers. |
| 2. Add oil drop by drop, stirring all the time as it thickens. | The emulsifiers form a film around the oil droplets. |
| 3. Slowly add vinegar or lemon juice. | This forms an oil-in-water emulsion. It also flavours and thins it to a coating consistency. |

Miscellaneous sauces

1. *Apple sauce*, served with roast pork, consists of apple purée slightly sweetened. It counteracts the richness of the meat.
2. *Bread sauce*, served with roast chicken, consists of white bread or crumbs simmered with onion and cloves in seasoned milk until creamy. It adds flavour and food value to the chicken.
3. *Mint sauce*, served with roast lamb, consists of finely chopped mint in sweetened vinegar. It adds flavour to the meat.
4. *Horseradish sauce*, served with roast beef consists of finely grated horseradish in cream or white sauce. It adds flavour and pungency to the meat.
5. *Jam, or marmalade sauce*, served with steamed or baked puddings is made by boiling jam (or marmalade) with sugar and water until a syrupy consistency is obtained. It moistens and flavours the puddings, and may be thickened with arrowroot if desired.

**Gravies**

Gravies are served with roast meats, and should be well flavoured with extractives from the meat itself. It is usual to serve a thin gravy with roast beef, pork, chicken and duck, and a thick gravy with lamb, veal, goose and turkey.

Thick gravy

| HOW | WHY |
|---|---|
| 1. Remove meat from roasting tin. | |
| Pour off nearly all fat. | Gravy must not be too greasy. |
| Retain the meat juices. | To give a good flavour. |
| 2. Add 1 rounded tablespoonful flour, mix well and cook over heat for 2–3 minutes. | To thicken. Starch grains swell, and absorb fat, and some starch may be dextrinised. |

| | |
|---|---|
| 3. Add 500 ml stock or vegetable water, stir until boiling. Boil 5 minutes. Season and strain. | To cook starch thoroughly and to develop flavour. |

Thin gravy

| HOW | WHY |
|---|---|
| 1. Pour off as much fat as possible. | To avoid greasiness. |
| 2. To the sediment, add 1 teaspoonful of flour, and 500 ml stock or vegetable water. | To give a smooth consistency. |
| 3. Boil for 2 minutes. | To cook starch thoroughly. |

## Seasonings, flavourings, accompaniments and garnishes

Seasonings

Seasonings are added to foods to bring out their natural flavourings, to make insipid foods appetising and to stimulate the flow of gastric juices.

1. *Salt*: obtained from brine.
a) It is a source of sodium and chlorine in the diet.
b) It helps to improve the natural flavours of foods.
c) It strengthens the gluten in flour mixtures.
d) It acts as a preservative for many foods.
Table salt usually has magnesium carbonate or sodium phosphate added to keep the salt dry, as salt itself is very hygroscopic, i.e. it absorbs water from the air. Iodised salt is useful in districts where the soil and water are deficient in iodine.

2. *Pepper*: is obtained from a tropical plant, the fruit of which is dried and ground. If the fruit is unripe, black pepper is obtained; if ripe, white pepper. Pepper contains an essential oil which stimulates the flow of digestive juices.
*Cayenne pepper* is made from ground dried chillies. It has a very strong flavour, and is used in curries, etc.
*Paprika pepper* is made from ground dried capsicum. It has a mild flavour and is used chiefly for its decorative red colour.

3. *Vinegar* is made by the action of bacteria on the alcohol of wine, cider or malt liquors. The alcohol is 'soured' or turned to acetic acid.
a) It is used to flavour fish, salads, etc.
b) It acts as a preservative, as micro-organisms cannot flourish in acid solutions.
c) It is used in cooking for sousing fish, marinating meat, etc.

4. *Lemons* supply both juice and the outer rind or 'zest'. Fresh lemon juice is an important source of vitamin C and when possible should be so used that the juice will not be heated.

Spices

*Spices* are now used to give extra flavour and variety to foods. In earlier times they were used to disguise disagreeable flavours.

1. *Ginger* is the underground stem of a tropical plant. It can be dried, preserved in syrup, or ground and used in cakes and puddings.
2. *Cinnamon* is the bark from the shoots of a tropical shrub. It is dried and used either in stick form or when ground to a powder.
3. *Cloves* are the flower buds of a tropical tree. The buds are dried and used whole in puddings, etc.
4. *Mixed spice* is a mixture of ground ginger, cinnamon and cloves.
5. *Capers* are the flower buds of a tropical shrub. They are pickled in salt and vinegar, and used in sauce.
6. *Celery seed* is the seed of the celery plant. It is ground and used in soups and stews.
7. *Caraway* is the seed of a plant. These seeds are dried and used to flavour cakes and buns.
8. *Nutmeg* is the kernel of the fruit of a tropical tree. These kernels are dried and grated on milk puddings, etc.
9. *Mace* is the outside husk of the fruit of the nutmeg tree. It is dried and powdered and used in stews and soups.
10. *Mustard* is made by grinding the seed of the mustard plant. Dried, it is used in pickles and chutneys; ground and mixed with water or vinegar it is used as a condiment.
11. *Chillies* are the dried pods of a species of capsicum or red pepper. They have a strong flavour and are used sparingly.
12. *Curry powder or paste* is a mixture of ginger, pepper, tumeric, chillies, nutmeg, etc., and is used in stews and curries.
13. *Allspice* comes from the ground, dried berries of the Jamaican pepper tree or pimento, and is used to flavour savoury dishes.
14. *Vanilla* is the seed pod of a tropical plant. The dried pod may be kept in a container of sugar to which it will impart a delicate flavour. An extract of vanilla in alcohol is used as a flavouring essence in cakes, puddings, etc.

Herbs

*Herbs* are plants containing pungent and fragrant essential oils. They are best used fresh and finely chopped. They may, however, be dried and powdered. Herbs supply flavour and, when fresh, also a little vitamin C. The most common herbs in use in England are mint, parsley, thyme, sage, marjoram, fennel, rosemary and chives. Bay leaves may be used fresh or dried and are usually added whole and removed before serving the food.

*Garlic* is the bulb of an onion-like plant. It has a very strong flavour, and should be used very sparingly.

*A bouquet garni* is a bunch of herbs, e.g. bay leaf, thyme, parsley, etc., tied in a small muslin bag with peppercorns. It is used to flavour soups and stews. It is cooked in the liquid and always removed before serving.

Flavourings
Colourings
Garnishes

1. *Flavouring essences:* these may be the essential oils of the plant dissolved in alcohol; more usually nowadays they are artificial chemical substances. Most are very volatile and are therefore better added after cooking. Examples are vanilla, lemon, almond, peppermint essences.
2. *Colourings* may be natural products (e.g. cochineal and saffron) or artificial dyes.
3. *Garnishes* are decorations added to savoury dishes just before serving to improve both appearance and flavour. They are usually edible, e.g. lemon slices with fish, chopped parsley with soup, parsley sprigs with any fried food. Sweet dishes are decorated, e.g. glacé cherries and nuts on trifle.

Stuffings and accompaniments

1. *Stuffings or forcemeat* are usually mixtures of breadcrumbs with some fat and herbs, e.g. sage and onion, lemon, parsley and thyme, chestnut. They add flavour and nourishment to meat, fish and poultry.
2. *Accompaniments* are served with dishes to add food value or to improve the colour, flavour and texture.

**Examples of accompaniments**

| *Dish* | *Accompaniment* |
|---|---|
| Thin soup | Shredded or diced vegetables, noodles or macaroni. |
| Thick soup | Fried or toasted bread croutons. |
| Fish: grilled or fried | Lemon slices, parsley butter, parsley, tomato or tartare sauce. |
| Fish: boiled, steamed or baked | Anchovy, cheese or parsley sauce, colourful vegetables. |
| Meat | Gravy or a sauce. Green or root vegetables, or a green salad. Potatoes. |
| Grilled or fried meat | Mushrooms, tomatoes, watercress, parsley butter. |
| Roast beef | Horseradish sauce, Yorkshire pudding, thin, brown gravy. |
| Roast lamb | Mint sauce or redcurrant jelly, thick, light brown gravy. |
| Roast pork or duck | Apple sauce and sage and onion stuffing, thick, light brown gravy. |
| Roast chicken | Bread sauce, bacon rolls. Chipolata sausages, parsley and thyme stuffing, thin, light brown gravy. |
| Steamed puddings and pies | Sweet or custard sauce. |
| Salads | Salad dressing or mayonnaise. |
| Vegetables (e.g. cauliflower) | White coating sauce or melted butter. |

# 15 Convenience foods

*Types of convenience foods  Advantages and disadvantages*
*What is in the packet?*

Convenience foods are those foods which are completely or partly prepared by the manufacturer. They are therefore easy or 'convenient' to use.

Nowadays, housewives do not spend as much time in the kitchen preparing food as they did a generation ago. Many women work outside the home and have little time for shopping and food preparation. It is usual to shop occasionally and to maintain stores of dried, canned and frozen foods which can be used to prepare a meal quickly. Less and less fresh food is bought daily, or weekly, thus most convenience foods are preserved to extend their shelf life. Ready-made dishes containing a variety of ingredients can now be purchased, saving time and effort. Some dishes which would require skill in preparation are very successful in the convenience form.

## Types of convenience foods

1. *Canned foods*: easy to store in a dry cupboard and will keep for a long time. They can be served cold, e.g. sardines, fruit, ham, or they can be used as part of a cooked dish. Many canned foods need re-heating only before serving, e.g. soups, vegetables, stewed meat, snack meals, as they are thoroughly cooked during processing.
2. *Dehydrated foods*: these are lightweight and easy to carry. Most store for up to a year in a dry cupboard. Small amounts can be reconstituted and the remainder used at another time, e.g. soup powders. Whole meals are available, e.g. rice and curry, paella, chow mein, and these are particularly useful for single people who do not have the time or the ingredients to prepare complicated dishes.

Some dehydrated foods can be reconstituted instantly, e.g. powdered coffee and milk. Instant puddings which are made up with fresh milk are quick, nutritious and easy to use. Instant savoury dishes, e.g. snackpots, need only boiling water added to produce hot, tasty food in the dish in which it was bought, – no washing up!

3. *Frozen foods*: these are probably nearest in quality to fresh foods, and most can be stored for at least a year in a freezer at −18°C. A wide variety of foods ready to cook are available, e.g. meat, poultry, fish, pastry goods, vegetables. Cooked dishes and complete meals need only to be thawed and re-heated. Ice-cream is an instant pudding from the freezer. Bread and cakes from the freezer are of good quality. Manufactured puff pastry is a

successful produce that would be difficult and time consuming to make oneself.

The principal disadvantage of some frozen foods is the length of time required to thaw large frozen pieces before cooking, although microwave ovens can reduce the time taken.

4. *Other processed foods*: ready-to-eat breakfast cereals, sliced bread, biscuits, cakes and puddings are all easy and quick to use.

Advantages of convenience foods

1. They save time in preparation.
2. They save labour.
3. They require little skill in preparation and cooking.
4. The quality is consistent.
5. There is no waste.
6. They can be stored in a cupboard or freezer for long periods.
7. They add variety to the diet.
8. Some foods are fortified with nutrients: e.g. cereals with B vitamins, evaporated milk with vitamins A and D.

Disadvantages

1. Some types of foods are expensive.
2. They may lack the flavour of untreated foods and should be used with discretion.
3. Vitamins B and C may be lost during processing

**What is in the packet?**

1. *Ingredients*: food manufacturers have to show on the packet a list of all the ingredients in descending order of weight. If there is a greater weight of rice than curry the dish must be called 'rice with curry', not 'curry with rice'. Where flavours, colours, emulsifiers, anti-oxidants and preservatives are used they need not be named but they must be of the permitted type. There are laws to control the standard of certain foods, e.g. ice-cream. There are many laws that ensure the consumer receives good value and quality when purchasing processed food. However, the cost of meeting all the required standards in factories and shops can increase the price of food significantly.

2. *Weight*: the weight and usually the number of portions are printed on the packet. In most types of foods there is no wastage and the price per portion can easily be calculated. Unit pricing on foods such as biscuits is helpful to price-conscious consumers. Packets may not appear filled because high speed packing machinery controls the weight but does not allow time for settling before sealing.

# 16 Preservation of fruit and vegetables

*Causes of decay Principles of preservation Methods used in the home*

Preservation of food is undertaken to prevent decay and to keep the food as fresh as possible.

Why food should be preserved

1. To deal with seasonal surplus and avoid waste, e.g. apples.
2. To provide 'out of season' food all the year, e.g. peas.
3. To make available from overseas foods not naturally found in this country, e.g. canned peaches.
4. As a means of meeting food demands of a nation where its own sources are insufficient, e.g. imported, frozen meat.
5. Convenience: frozen and canned foods are quick and easy to prepare.

**Causes of decay**

1. *Enzymes* in the food itself, i.e. chemical substances which act as catalysts and speed up chemical changes which would, otherwise, proceed very slowly. An example of these changes is the browning of some fruit when cut and exposed to air. Enzymes work quickly in warm conditions but more slowly in cold. They are inactivated by heat, e.g. in blanching vegetables. They are not harmful but they bring about changes in flavour, colour and nutritive value that are undesirable.
2. *Micro-organisms*, i.e. minute forms of life which get into food or on to its surface and which need warmth, moisture and, usually, air for their growth. Micro-organisms are of three classes:
a) Moulds which grow on the surface of food.
b) Yeasts which grow in the presence of sugar.
c) Bacteria which attack and break down proteins, fats and carbohydrates.

**Principles of preservation**

The following scientific principles underly all methods of preservation; one or more of them may be applied in each case:
1. To destroy by heat any enzymes or micro-organisms in the food.
2. To prevent the enzymes or micro-organisms causing deterioration:
a) by removing air or water, *or*
b) by reducing the temperature, *or*
c) by using a strong concentration of sugar, salt or vinegar, *or*
d) by the use of chemical preserving agents.

3. To prevent the further access of micro-organisms to the food by careful storage, e.g. in tins or tightly sealed jars.

**Methods of preservation**
1. *Drying or dehydration*: the removal of water prevents the action of enzymes and micro-organisms, e.g. dried apple rings, herbs.
2. *Cold storage*: this prevents decay as the organisms are inactive below a certain temperature, e.g. in the storage of food for short periods in a domestic refrigerator, or for long periods in a deep-freeze cabinet.
3. *Jam and jelly making*: the cooking destroys the enzymes and micro-organisms, and the 60 per cent sugar solution reduces the water activity so preventing the growth of any micro-organisms which may enter from the air.
4. *Bottling and canning*: the heating destroys the micro-organisms and enzymes initially present, and the air-tight seal prevents the entry of any other micro-organisms from the air.
5. *Pickling*: the heating destroys the enzymes and micro-organisms initially present, and the vinegar, being acid, prevents the growth of any which may enter the bottle or jar later.
6. *Salting*: the salt has two effects: the micro-organisms cannot extract the water they need for growth from strong salt solutions, and also a high concentration of salt is toxic to them.
7. *Addition of a chemical preservative*, e.g. Campden tablets which produce sulphur dioxide. This destroys the micro-organisms and enzymes in the first place, and the weak solution remains sterile in a sealed jar.

*Dried apple rings*

| HOW | WHY | |
|---|---|---|
| 1. Wash, peel and core apples, cut into ½ cm slices. | To remove dirt. To expose maximum surface area. | 1 Drying |
| 2. Put into salt solution for 10 minutes. (1 level tablespoon salt to 1 litre water.) | Colour is preserved, water from fruit is drawn out by osmosis. | |
| 3. Rinse well and dry. | To remove taste of salt. | |
| 4. Thread on strings and hang in a warm place at 60°C. | To allow remaining water to evaporate, thus stopping enzyme action. | |
| 5. When they have the texture of chamois leather, store in a covered jar in a cool, dry, dark place. | They are dehydrated enough to prevent the growth of micro-organisms. | |
| 6. Before use, soak in water for 24 hours. | To replace the water removed by drying. | |

**2 Freezing**

Freezing is suitable for preserving meat, poultry, vegetables and fruits. It is discussed in greater detail in the next Chapter (page 131).

**3 Jam making**

*Qualities of good jam*

1. Distinct fruity taste. This depends on the quality of the fruit.
2. Clear with a bright colour. This depends on the acid content.
3. Well set but not too stiff. This depends on the pectin (see below) and the acid content, and on the length of time of boiling.
4. Good keeping properties. This depends on the sugar content which should be about 60 per cent.

*Principles of jam making*

1. Fruit contains a gum-like substance called *pectin*, and also a certain amount of acid. When sugar, pectin and acid are present in the correct proportions and the jam is boiled it will set, or 'gel', on cooling.
2. Some fruits (apples, blackcurrants, gooseberries, plums and all citrus fruits) are rich in pectin and acid and will easily make jams, jellies or marmalades. Other fruits (cherries, melons, strawberries) are poor in pectin and acid. When these are made into jam, extra acid in the form of lemon juice may be needed to help the jam set; or they can be mixed with a fruit rich in pectin; or commercial pectin may be used.
3. The fruit is simmered in the first stage of jam making to soften it, to release the pectin and to destroy the enzymes and micro-organisms present.
4. Sugar is then added and should be in the proportion of about 6 parts of sugar, by weight, to 10 parts of the finished jam. Micro-organisms cannot grow in this concentration of sugar.
5. The jam is boiled quickly to make it set, and to hydrolyse some of the added sucrose to glucose and fructose ('invert' sugar). This helps to prevent crystallisation.
6. The jam is put in jars and covered to discourage the entry of micro-organisms from the air. It is then stored in a cool, dry place.

*To make jam*:

| HOW | WHY |
|---|---|
| 1. Choose fruit which is just ripe and still firm. | At this stage it contains the greatest amount of pectin. |
| 2. Weigh, wash and place (with water if necessary) in large preserving pan. | A large pan gives the greatest area for evaporation. |
| 3. Simmer fruit slowly. | To soften the fruit and to release the pectin. |
| 4. Add acid if necessary. | To help to release the pectin. |

| | |
|---|---|
| 5. Add sugar and stir with a wooden spoon, 1 kg sugar to 1 kg fruit is the average. Fruits rich in pectin will take more sugar. | |
| 6. Allow to boil rapidly. | To hydrolyse some of the added sugar and to reach setting point. |
| 7. Stir occasionally. | To prevent sticking and burning. |
| 8. Test for setting after about 10 minutes by: | |
| a) Taking up some boiling jam on a wooden spoon, cooling it slightly and pouring it back into the pan, *or* | The cooled jam does not fall in a thin stream but breaks into flakes as it begins to set. |
| b) Using a thermometer to check that the temperature is 105°C, *or* | A 60% sugar solution boils at 105°C. |
| c) Placing a little jam on a cold plate and leaving it to cool. When the jam sets the surface wrinkles when pushed with a finger. | A small amount of jam cools quickly and can be used to test the 'set'. |

## 4 Bottling

Bottling is a process in which fruit is packed into clean bottles or jars and covered with water or syrup. The jars are then sterilised, and sealed with special tops to prevent the entry of air. Canning (which is not normally carried out in the home) depends on the same principles but the cans are sealed before sterilisation.

*Principles of bottling*

1. Fruit is heated slowly in the jars, either in the oven or in a pan of water, so that the enzymes and micro-organisms are destroyed but the fruit remains whole.
2. While still hot, the jars are sealed. The partial vacuum formed under the lid as the contents cool keeps the seal firm and prevents the entry of micro-organisms from the air.
3. The jars are stored in a cool, dark, dry place, thus providing conditions in which micro-organisms do not flourish.

*To bottle fruit:*

| **HOW** | **WHY** |
|---|---|
| 1. Choose fruit that is firm and just ripe. | Such fruit will keep its shape and is less likely to decay than over-ripe fruit. |
| 2. Prepare and wash as for stewing. | |
| 3. Prepare a syrup of about 250 g sugar to 500 ml water. Boil, cool. | Syrup sweetens fruit and improves the flavour. |

| | |
|---|---|
| 4. Choose jars which are sound, clean and with well-fitting lids. | To ensure an airtight seal. |
| 5. *Either* a) Pack fruit tightly into wet jars and fill to the top with syrup. | Fruit shrinks in cooking and will rise in the jars unless tightly packed. |
| Place in a pan on a thick cloth, with cold water up to the necks of the jars. | |
| Place the lids lightly on the jars and *slowly* raise the temperature to 90°C (simmering point) in about ½ hour. Keep soft fruits at this temperature for 2 minutes, hard fruits for 10 minutes. | Heat destroys the enzymes and micro-organisms and fruit should remain whole if heating is slow. |
| Screw or clip down lid immediately. | To prevent entry of air and to create a partial vacuum as the jars cool. |
| *or* b) Pack fruit into jars but do not add the syrup. Place jars in a slow oven (150°C, Gas 2) and heat slowly. As the fruit shrinks, fill up the jars with fruit from a spare jar. Soft fruit takes ½ hour, hard fruit longer. When cooked, remove one jar at a time, fill with boiling syrup and place on the lids and screw tops at once. | |
| 6. Cool for 24 hours and then test for a seal by removing screw or clip and lifting jar by the lid. | To make sure that no air can enter. |
| 7. If seal is firm, store in a cool dry place. | |

*Bottling of vegetables*

This should not be attempted without a pressure cooker because, unlike fruit, vegetables are non-acid. Food poisoning bacteria known as *Clostridium botulinum* are able to produce spores in non-acid conditions at high temperatures and so survive normal bottling conditions. By using a pressure cooker with a medium weight, a temperature of 115.3°C can be reached, which is sufficient to preserve vegetables safely. However, great care should be taken as faulty processing can result in food poisoning. Pressure cooker manufacturers provide detailed instructions for vegetable bottling and these should be followed very carefully.

5 Pickling and chutney making

In these preserves, vinegar is an important ingredient as it contains 5% acetic acid which inhibits the development of micro-organisms. Spices, sugar and salt add flavour and aid preservation.

*Pickling* (onions, red cabbage, cucumbers, etc.)

| HOW | WHY |
|---|---|
| 1. Prepare vegetables as for cooking. Cut if necessary. | For convenience in packing. |
| 2. Soak for 24 hours in brine (100 g salt to 500 ml water). | To reduce water content of vegetables by osmosis. |
| 3. Rinse and drain. | To remove excess salt. |
| 4. Pack into jars, leaving 1 cm space at top. | To allow vinegar to cover vegetables completely. |
| 5. Heat 1 litre vinegar with 25 g pickling spice and allow to cool. | For added flavour. |
| 6. Pour vinegar into jars. | Vinegar enters vegetables, thus replacing their water content. |
| 7. Cover tightly with non-metal covers. | To prevent evaporation.<br>To prevent acid attacking the cover. |

*Chutney making* (apple, gooseberry, tomato, marrow, etc.)

| HOW | WHY |
|---|---|
| 1. Cut or mince ingredients into small pieces. | To make it easier to pulp. |
| 2. Cook in a little water until soft. | Cellulose will not soften easily in acid conditions. |
| 3. Add vinegar, spices and sugar and cook gently until thick. | To reduce the water content and to blend the flavours. |
| 4. Bottle in hot jars. | To prevent cracking of jars. |
| 5. Cover as for pickles. | |

In this process water passes from the food by osmosis and is replaced by the salt solution, e.g. salting of meat or fish by placing between layers of dry salt or in a solution of brine, salting of runner beans in dry salt.

## 6 Salting

*Salting of runner beans:*

| HOW | WHY |
|---|---|
| 1. Slice beans as for cooking. | To expose a large area to the salt. |
| 2. Arrange a layer of salt on the bottom of an earthenware or glass container. Place on this a 2 cm layer of beans. | Salt prevents the action of enzymes and micro-organisms. |
| 3. Repeat with alternate layers of dry salt and beans, finishing with a layer of salt. | |
| 4. Fill the jar the next day with further layers as beans sink. | Water extracted from the beans dissolves some of the salt. |
| 5. Cover and store in a cool, dark, dry place. | To prevent loss of colour. |

To use salted beans, soak for 1 to 2 hours, drain and cook in water without salt.

## 7 Chemical preservation

Campden tablets which produce sulphur dioxide can be used for preserving certain fruits such as apples and plums by following the instructions supplied with the tablets.

| HOW | WHY |
|---|---|
| 1. Prepare fruit as for stewing. | For convenience in packing. |
| 2. Pack into preserving jars. | |
| 3. Crush Campden tablets and dissolve in cold water. Pour on to fruit. | Sulphur dioxide is produced. Micro-organisms and enzymes are destroyed. |
| 4. Cover and store in a cool dry place. | To prevent vaporisation of sulphur dioxide. |

To use fruit preserved in this way, put the fruit into a saucepan without a lid and boil gently until all the sulphur dioxide is driven off. Sweeten to taste.

# 17 Home freezing

*Choice of freezer  Using a freezer  Principles of preservation by freezing  Methods of home freezing  Packing  Storage  Thawing*

## Choice of freezer

Upright or chest type freezers are available and the choice may depend on the amount of floor space available.

Types of freezer

An upright freezer has a door and shelves with baskets, so the food is easily accessible. However, when the door is opened cold air escapes so this type of freezer tends to be less efficient and less economical. Upright freezers are available as combined fridge-freezers.

A chest freezer has a counterbalanced lid and the cold air does not escape when it is opened. The depth of the storage compartment may make foods at the bottom inaccessible, especially when the chest is fully loaded, but wire baskets which slide across the top partly overcome this problem.

The size of freezer required will depend on the number of people it is serving and thus on the amount of fruit and vegetables, meat, fish or pre-cooked convenience foods that will be stored. The freezer should bear the symbol [* ***] which indicates that fresh foods may be frozen. Cabinets which merely store pre-frozen foods bear the symbol [***].

## Using a freezer

It should be installed in a cool, dry, well-ventilated place. It should contain a thermometer to be used for checking that the temperature remains below −18°C (0°F). The fast-freeze switch should be used to reduce the temperature of the freezer two hours before freezing any quantity of fresh food. Fresh food up to one-tenth of the total capacity of the freezer can be frozen in 24 hours, any more than this leads to slow freezing and warming of the stored foods. Defrosting should be carried out once or twice a year, as necessary. In the event of breakdown or a power cut, food in the freezer will remain in good condition for up to 8 hours provided the freezer is not opened.

Advantages of a freezer

1. To store surplus fruit and vegetables from the garden.
2. To store bulk purchases of meat, fish, fruit or vegetables bought at economical prices.
3. To store home-cooked foods, e.g. pies, bread, casseroles, for parties, emergencies or holidays.
4. To store convenience products for quick meals, e.g. fish fingers, ice-cream.

5. To reduce waste: single portions can be prepared or left-overs can be kept.

Disadvantages of a freezer

1. The cost of storage, i.e. cost of freezer, packaging and fuel.
2. Stock control: frozen food does not keep unchanged forever. Foods should be used within a certain time limit (see page 134).
3. Frozen food lacks the subtle textures and flavours of well prepared fresh foods, so it should be used with discretion.
4. A considerable loss of food may occur if a breakdown is not detected within 24 hours.

**The principles of preserving food by freezing**

Food is preserved at low temperatures because enzyme activity and the growth of micro-organisms are reduced. At temperatures below −18°C, most enzymes are so inactive that they cause no further deterioration in the food. Low temperatures do not kill micro-organisms, but in frozen food free water is no longer available for micro-organisms to grow and multiply or for enzyme reactions to take place; the water is 'tied up' in ice crystals.

If food is quick-frozen many small ice crystals form, if it is frozen slowly then larger ice crystals develop. The large ice crystals spoil the texture of the food because they break cell walls, disrupt tissues and withdraw water from proteins. The food then loses its succulence and much 'drip' is lost during thawing or cooking.

**Methods of home freezing**

Meat

All freshly slaughtered meat carcasses must be hung in a cool place until tender. The meat is then cut into suitable sized joints or portions. Any excess fat or bones should be removed. Some pieces of meat can be trimmed and minced prior to freezing. Spare fat can be rendered down for dripping.

All meat should be closely wrapped in moisture-vapour proof film, e.g. polythene, otherwise 'freezer burn' could occur: the ice turns to water vapour and evaporates from the surface of the meat leaving a whitish 'scar' where it dries.

Bacon is best vacuum-packed before freezing otherwise it tends to go rancid.

Fish

Fish must be freshly caught if it is to be home frozen, otherwise it is better to buy commercially frozen fish. Fresh fish should be gutted, washed and dried before freezing.

Eggs

Fresh eggs are best beaten or separated before freezing. Hard boiled eggs are unsuitable for freezing as they become tough and watery.

Cheese

Cheese that is fully mature freezes well, although it may be a little crumbly after thawing. Grated cheese freezes well.

**Milk, yoghurt, cream**

Homogenised milk can be frozen but other types separate. Never freeze milk in a glass bottle. Sweetened yoghurt with fruit can be frozen. Double cream freezes successfully and it can be whipped first and piped into rosettes.

**Bread**

Fresh bread freezes well. Sliced bread can be toasted from frozen. Breadcrumbs, to be used for stuffings, can conveniently be stored in the freezer. Most sandwiches freeze well but avoid fillings of hard boiled egg, salad or salad cream, and bananas.

**Cakes and pastry**

Most cakes freeze well, either undecorated or iced. Iced and cream cakes can be open-frozen and covered when they are hard. They should be uncovered before thawing or condensation will spoil the decoration.

Most pastry can be frozen either unbaked or baked, only choux pastry needs cooking first.

**Fruits**

Fruits contain acids which help to prevent enzymes and micro-organisms from causing spoilage. Only good quality, firm, dry fruit should be frozen and this may be done in the following ways:

1. Without additions, e.g. gooseberries, orange and grapefruit segments.
2. With sugar, e.g. rhubarb (add 100 g sugar to 400 g fruit).
3. In sugar syrup, e.g. sliced peaches. The syrup can vary in sweetness, between 200 g – 2 kg sugar per litre of water. To prevent browning of fruit by oxidation, ascorbic acid can be added to the syrup (½ teaspoon or 150 mg per litre).
4. As a purée, e.g. blackcurrants, cooked or uncooked, sieved and sweetened if desired. This is a compact way of storing fruit and is useful for sauces, soufflés or sorbets.

Bananas and pears do not freeze well.

**Vegetables**

Vegetables are not acid like fruits; the enzymes they contain work slowly, even at low temperatures, and colour, flavour and nutritional value deteriorate. To prevent this, vegetables are cut into small pieces and heat-treated to inactivate the enzymes, – this is called blanching. Small quantities of vegetables are plunged into fast boiling water, covered and quickly returned to the boil for 1–3 minutes. They are then cooled in ice cold water, drained and packed for freezing. (A salad spinner is useful for removing any excess cold water.)

Vegetables with a low water content, e.g. peas, freeze most successfully. Salad vegetables, e.g. lettuce and cucumber, do not retain a suitable texture after freezing. Tomatoes can be frozen if they are to be served cooked.

## Packaging of frozen foods

Packaging materials used for frozen foods should provide a barrier to prevent loss of moisture, to exclude oxygen and to prevent the tainting of foods by odours. The material used must be strong and flexible so that it is not easily damaged and must seal easily. It should be unaffected by the acids, fats or water in foods.

Materials

Heavy gauge polythene may be used as bags or use semi-rigid containers, e.g. Tupperware. Saranwrap is another type of plastic film which clings to food and is heat-sealable. Polypropylene is used to make boil-in-the-bag pouches, e.g. for kipper fillets. Cellophane is used to separate individual portions within a container. Waxed cartons are suitable for some foods, e.g. soups. Heavy duty aluminium foil is a very effective packaging material, although it is best laminated with polythene or paper to prevent puncturing. Foil dishes in a variety of shapes and sizes are useful for baked goods.

Sealing

This is necessary to prevent loss of moisture from foods that are stored for a long time. Plastic coated wires or freezer tape can be used. Some plastics can be heat sealed by a warm iron used over this paper. Reducing the amount of air in contact with the food helps to reduce oxidation. Oxidation causes undesirable changes in colour, flavour and nutritional value. Fats and foods such as oily fish and pork develop rancid flavours in the presence of air and should not be stored for too long. Air may be sucked out of bags, or food may be close-wrapped in film or foil.

Labelling

All food needs to be labelled in order to identify it: for example, when wrapped it is not easy to recognise different cuts of frozen meat. The weight or number of portions should be recorded on the label, also the date on which it was frozen. Special labels and pens need to be used to withstand moisture and low temperatures.

## Storage of frozen foods

The most important factor in storage is to maintain a constant temperature of −18°C. Fluctuations in temperature, caused by frequent opening of the freezer, or overloading with fresh food, allow the ice crystals to increase in size and so spoil the texture of frozen foods. Oxidative rancidity spoils many fatty foods if stored too long. However, many people are not critical of minor changes in colour, texture or flavour of foods and most foods may be safely eaten even if the maximum storage time has elapsed. The following table is a guide for maximum length of storage:

Storage times

| | |
|---|---|
| Bacon and cured meats | 1 month |
| Minced meat and offal | 3 months |
| Prepared dishes | 3 months |
| Oily fish, e.g. mackerel | 3 months |
| Pork | 4–6 months |
| Cheese | 6 months |

| | |
|---|---|
| White fish, e.g. cod | 6 months |
| Eggs | 9 months |
| Fruit | 9–12 months |
| Beef, lamb, chicken | 9–12 months |
| Vegetables | 10–12 months |

**Thawing of frozen foods**

Once foods have thawed they should be cooked or consumed immediately. Many cells are damaged in thawed foods, so they are particularly prone to spoilage by the enzymes and micro-organisms which become active at normal temperatures. If possible, uncooked foods are best thawed slowly in a refrigerator so that little water is lost as 'drip'.

Some foods are best cooked from the frozen state without thawing, e.g vegetables, fruits, thin pieces of fish.

It is most important to completely thaw poultry and large pieces of boned and rolled meat which may be contaminated with food poisoning bacteria. If the meat is still frozen at the centre, normal cooking will not raise the temperature at the centre sufficiently to kill the harmful bacteria. Prepared meat dishes, e.g. casseroles and stews, must be thawed and thoroughly re-heated for the same reason.

# 18 Kitchen hygiene

*Food spoilage   Food contamination   Larders   Refrigerators*

Correct hygiene in the kitchen is of great importance because upon it depends the health of the family. Food must be correctly handled and stored, in order to:
1. Avoid spoilage in appearance or taste, otherwise the food becomes unpalatable.
2. Avoid contamination, otherwise food becomes harmful to eat.

## Food spoilage

Reasons for food spoilage

1. By becoming too dry, e.g. green vegetables wilt, fruit and root vegetables shrivel.
2. By becoming too wet, e.g. sugar goes lumpy; crisp foods, such as biscuits, go soft.
3. By the action of enzymes in the foods themselves, e.g. fruit rots and changes colour.
4. By the action of micro-organisms from the air, e.g. moulds on the surface of bread and jam, yeasts in fermenting fruit juices and bottled fruit, bacteria in the souring of milk, putrefaction of fish and meat. (See also Chapter 16.)
5. By animal or insect pests, e.g. weevils in cereals.

How to prevent food spoilage

1. By storing food, whether raw or cooked, under the most suitable conditions (see also under individual foods).
a) Meat, milk, butter and cheese in covered containers in a cool place.
b) Vegetables in a well-ventilated rack in a cool, dark place; salad vegetables in a covered container, or in a polythene bag in a refrigerator.
c) Bread in a ventilated bin, cakes and biscuits in separate tins.
d) Dry stores in glass, earthenware or plastic containers with lids, kept in a dark, cool place.
e) Tinned goods in a dry, cool place.
2. By planning the larder properly, and by the intelligent use of a refrigerator. If there is a refrigerator and a dry store cupboard there is no real need for a larder.

## Food contamination

How food becomes contaminated

Sometimes tainted food may be quite indistinguishable from wholesome food in taste and appearance, but it has become contaminated in some way so that if eaten it causes symptoms of food poisoning, e.g. stomach pains, vomiting, diarrhoea. This 'contaminated' food must not be confused with food which has been spoilt by poor storage.

Food poisoning may be caused by:

1. Certain poisonous foods, e.g. berries or fungi. (Some people are allergic to certain foods, i.e. they react to ordinary foods such as strawberries, shell-fish, or eggs, which do not affect other people.)
2. Certain metallic substances present in the food, e.g. arsenic from fruit sprays, zinc from galvanised vessels used for cooking.
3. The presence of harmful bacteria in the food:
a) *Salmonellae* bacteria from the intestines of man and animals.
b) *Staphylococci* present in the nose and throat, and in septic cuts, boils, etc. These form a toxin which contaminates food.
c) Miscellaneous bacteria causing similar symptoms.
d) *Clostridium botulinum* bacteria which cause botulism and are rare but very dangerous. The spores are resistant to heat. The bacilli produce toxins which have a serious effect on the central nervous system.

*Foods most likely to cause food poisoning*:
1. Meat and made-up meat dishes, e.g. sausages, brawn, pies.
2. Milk and milk dishes, e.g. synthetic cream, ice-cream.
3. Soups, gravies, stews.
4. Eggs (particularly ducks' eggs).
5. Fish.

The following conditions encourage the growth of food-poisoning bacteria: warmth, moisture and air. Bacteria multiply very rapidly; time is therefore an important factor.

How to prevent food contamination

1. *By paying attention to personal hygiene*
a) Frequent hand washing, particularly after use of lavatory.
b) Covering all cuts and sores with clean dressings.
c) Not coughing or sneezing near food.
d) Wearing clean overalls and hair coverings.
e) Not handling food unnecessarily.
f) Not working with food when one has a cold or a stomach upset.

The above points should apply to all who handle food.

2. *By cleanliness of kitchen premises and equipment*
a) All working surfaces must be clean and in good repair.
b) Kitchen must be kept free from pests, e.g. mice, flies, cockroaches.
c) Pets must not be allowed near human food.
d) Washing-up must be done in really hot water and all utensils should be rinsed well before being left to dry in a rack.
e) If drying cloths are used they must be spotlessly clean.
f) All dish cloths, tea towels, mops, etc. must be washed regularly.

Dilute bleach is an effective and useful disinfectant in the kitchen, it can be washed off and leaves no residual smell or taste.

3. *By care over the disposal of waste*
a) All decayable rubbish must be kept in covered containers

which are frequently emptied and washed out.
b) Dustbins must be tightly covered, kept away from the windows of the kitchen, and regularly emptied, cleaned and disinfected.
4. *By care over the storage of foods*
General rule: 'Keep food clean, cool and covered'. It is best to use a refrigerator or a ventilated larder.
a) *Meat*: keep covered and as cool as possible in a refrigerator or a cool larder. Use soon after buying. Do not partly cook meat one day and finish cooking later; any bacteria not killed by heat at the first stage will multiply rapidly in the warm meat. This is particularly important in large boned and rolled joints where food poisoning bacteria from outside may contaminate the centre of the joint. Large pieces of frozen meat must be completely thawed before cooking, otherwise the outside will overcook before the centre has reached a safe temperature. The drip from thawing meat must not contaminate other foods. Boards and knives used for fresh meat should not be used for cooked meats or cross-contamination will occur. Raw meat is frequently a source of food poisoning bacteria and all meats are a good medium for their growth.
b) *Milk*: keep in a refrigerator or in the coolest possible place. Never leave milk standing in the sun, as ultra-violet light destroys riboflavin (vitamin $B_2$) and ascorbic acid (vitamin C). If no refrigerator is available, scald milk in very hot weather if intending to keep it overnight.(Heat kills the *Lactobacilli*.)
c) *Left-overs*: keep covered in a cool place, use as soon as possible. Boil soups, gravies, stews, etc. before serving them again.
d) *Fish* is difficult to keep fresh; it should be put in a covered container in a refrigerator to keep it overnight in warm weather.

## The larder

| | HOW | WHY |
|---|---|---|
| Planning a larder | 1. Position should be near kitchen on outside wall, if possible on north or north-east side. | For convenience.<br>To keep as cool as possible. |
| | 2. Must have ventilation, if possible by window on outside wall. | To keep air fresh. |
| | 3. Window should be covered with a fly screen. | To keep out flies and other pests when window is open. |
| | 4. Should have well placed electric lighting. | For convenience at night. |
| | 5. Walls and ceiling should be smooth, in good repair, and light in colour. | For easy cleaning.<br>For good illumination. |

| | |
|---|---|
| 6. Floors should be smooth and cool, made of materials such as vinyl tiles or quarry tiles. | For easy cleaning. |
| 7. Shelving should be shallow, easily reached and covered with a washable surface. | For convenience in storage, and for easy cleaning. |
| 8. A vegetable rack is useful in the larder. | Circulation of air prevents vegetables sweating and rotting. |
| 9. All foods must be stored on clean plates or in clean containers. Use left-over foods as soon as possible. | To prevent contamination, and growth of micro-organisms. |
| 10. All food stored in the larder must be used in turn, old stock used before new stock. | All foods have a limited shelf life and deteriorate with time. |
| 11. The larder must be kept scrupulously clean. | |

## Refrigerators

The low temperature of a refrigerator enables perishable food to be kept for several days, as it reduces the activity of micro-organisms and enzymes which cause deterioration. Usually the temperature is kept at between 5°C and 8°C (40°F and 45°F) in the main part; in the ice box it is about −9°C (15°F). The low temperature is produced by a device in which liquid is made to evaporate, taking heat from its surroundings as it does so. Afterwards the gas thus produced is cooled and condensed for use again.

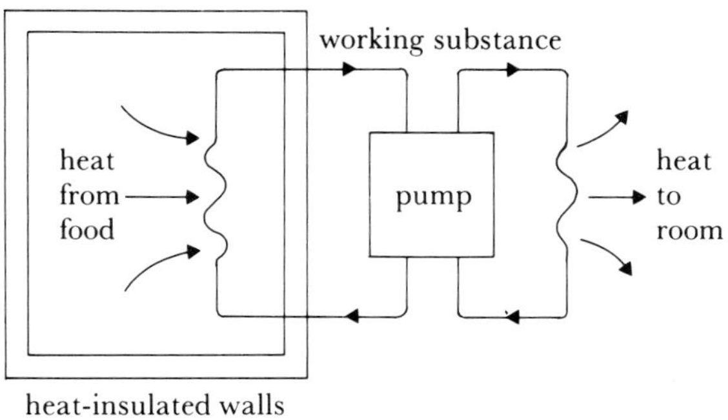


*How a refrigerator works*

How a refrigerator works

When the refrigerating liquid (or working substance) evaporates to form gas in the freezing unit, heat is taken from the food in the refrigerator. The gas is compressed by a motor or pump, the

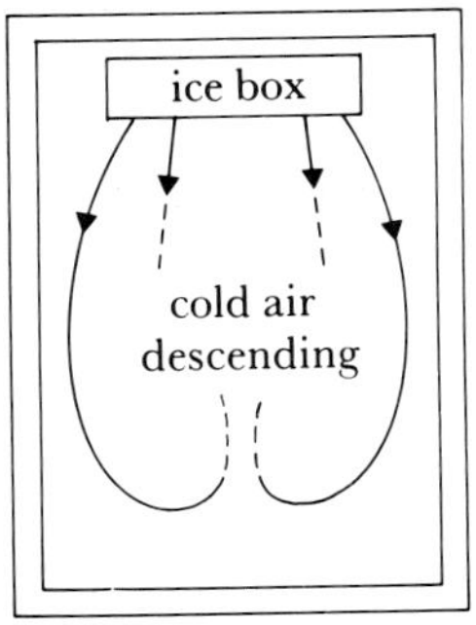


*Circulation of air in a refrigerator*

working liquid is reformed and heat is given off to the outside air. The refrigerator should therefore not be fitted in an enclosed space.

A refrigerator may be run by electricity, gas or paraffin. It consists of a double walled cabinet, usually of pressed steel, finished with vitreous enamel, with the space between the layers filled with heat-insulating material, such as glass fibre. The freezing unit (ice box) is usually at the top of the cabinet. Air circulates inside the refrigerator. It is cooled near the ice box and falls to the bottom of the cabinet, taking heat from the contents. The warmer air at the bottom is pushed up again by the heavy cold air coming down (convection currents).

Use and care of the refrigerator

| HOW | WHY |
|---|---|
| 1. As the temperature is controlled by a thermostat, set the control at a number which will keep the temperature of the cabinet at 5°C. | For economy of fuel. |
| 2. Pack foods carefully but not tightly together. | To allow free circulation of air. |
| 3. Pack foods in correct position as suggested by the manufacturer's chart. | To make best use of low temperatures. |
| 4. Always cover foods (polythene bags or film are useful). | Foods will become dry and flavours mixed if left uncovered. |
| 5. Always allow food to cool before putting in refrigerator. | Hot food slightly raises the temperature of the interior. This is wasteful of fuel. |
| 6. Clean and defrost regularly, unless it automatically defrosts itself. | Deposit of frost forms round freezing unit. This will reduce efficiency. |
| 7. Avoid opening door more than necessary. | This wastes fuel. |

*Storage of frozen food in a refrigerator*

Stars marked on the outside of a refrigerator indicate the temperature maintained in the frozen food compartment and consequently the length of storage time for frozen food.

* −6°C up to 1 week
** −12°C up to 1 month
*** −18°C up to 3 months

*Defrosting and cleaning*

1. Turn the thermostat to the index mark specified in the maker's instructions.

2. Remove all food and leave door open.
3. Place drip tray under the freezing unit.
4. Remove ice trays, empty and refill with fresh water.
5. Remove shelves, wash in warm water and dry well.
6. When all frost has melted, clean inside cabinet with clean water and mild detergent.
7. Wipe the outside with a clean, damp cloth.
8. Polish any chromium fittings with a soft, dry cloth.
9. Turn thermostat control to required number, replace food and close door.
10. When leaving the house with the power turned off (as when going on holiday), switch off the refrigerator and leave the door of the refrigerator open to ensure free circulation of air. This will prevent mould forming.

# 19 Kitchen planning

*Kitchen layout   Cookers, types and choices   Sinks   Working surfaces   Electrical equipment   Small equipment   Weighing and measuring*

## Kitchen layout

The kitchen should be an efficient and pleasant workshop. A good kitchen should be:

1. Conveniently placed in the house (not like the Victorian basement).
2. Planned to save time and effort.
3. Easy to keep clean and free from steam and grease.
4. Planned for the safety of the occupants, with special precautions where children are in the family.

When planning a kitchen the following points should be considered:

Planning a kitchen

| HOW | WHY |
|---|---|
| *Aspect*<br>The kitchen is probably best facing east with, if possible, an open view from the window. | To give morning sunshine and to prevent a feeling of isolation. |
| *Position in the house*<br>Near dining area and near back door. | For general convenience and to avoid walking long distances. |
| *Size*<br>This depends on the way in which it is used. If it is merely a workroom, about 8 sq m is a reasonable area. If it is used for meals also, about 12 sq m is better. | Too large a room wastes time and energy, and too small a room is cramping to work in and difficult to keep tidy. |
| *Shape*<br>A rectangular shape is probably better than a square. | For a given area this gives longer wall space where equipment can be placed. |
| *Position of doors*<br>Doors should not be on opposite walls nor placed so that they foul each other when opened. | To avoid draughts and accidents. |

| **HOW** | **WHY** |
| --- | --- |
| *Position of the main equipment* | |
| Cooker and sink should be close together with working surfaces near both, and if possible near window. | To avoid unnecessary steps. To give good light. |
| Storage for food and utensils should be near sink and cooker. | |
| There should be a flat surface near the door. | To receive shopping and parcels from outside. |

*A well-planned kitchen*

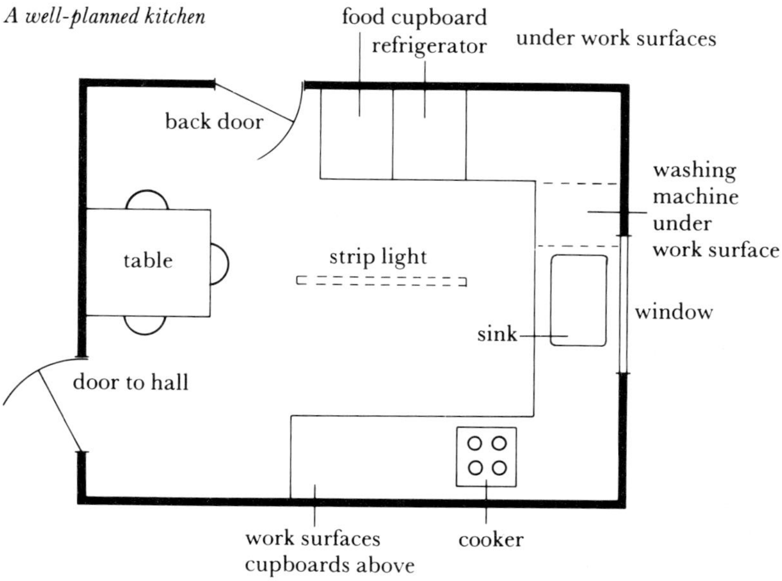


| | |
| --- | --- |
| *Lighting* | |
| Windows should be large and not too high. Artificial lighting must be well placed to give adequate light over all main working positions. | To ease the work and to make accidents less likely. |
| *Ventilation* | |
| This must be thoroughly efficient. It is usually provided by doors and windows but probably the best method of ventilation is by an electric extractor fan. | To get rid of steam and food smells and to ensure a supply of fresh air. |
| *Space heating* | |
| This must be adequate. Solid fuel cookers or water heaters also warm the kitchen. Oil, electric or gas radiators may be used. | Comfort of the worker is essential although kitchens vary greatly in the amount of heating required. |
| Avoid portable heaters and trailing flexes. | These are dangerous, as they may cause falls. |

| HOW | WHY |
|---|---|
| *Walls*<br>These should be smooth, light in colour and easily cleaned. There are many suitable wall surfaces available. | Constant cleaning is necessary. Light walls reflect light. |
| *Floors*<br>Floor coverings should be chosen from the wide range of modern products available. Consider such points as ease of cleaning, durability, resilience, warmth, freedom from slipperiness, as well as cost and appearance. | Floors require constant cleaning; they should therefore be resistant to dirt and easily cleaned. |
| *Position of storage areas*<br>Cooking pans, tools and utensils should be near the cooker and working surfaces (table, etc.). Cleaning materials near sink.<br><br>Food: Fresh vegetables near sink.<br><br>Dry goods near working surface.<br><br>Perishable goods in a refrigerator, or a ventilated larder. | To save unnecessary work in carrying. |
| *Position of laundry equipment*<br>Washing machine, spin dryer should be near the sink and near power plugs. They can be under the working surface. | |
| *Safety precautions*<br>Arrange good lighting. Store everything needed within easy reach. Avoid traffic through kitchen when possible. Provide adequate supervision of children and old people.<br><br>Provide adequate first aid box. | The most common accidents in the kitchen are burns, scalds, cuts and falls. |
| *Colour scheme*<br>This is entirely a personal matter but the kitchen decor should provide a light, cheerful background. | The kitchen should provide the best working environment possible. |

*Working surfaces, cupboards and shelves*
Arrange so that they are at the correct height, easy to reach and conveniently spaced

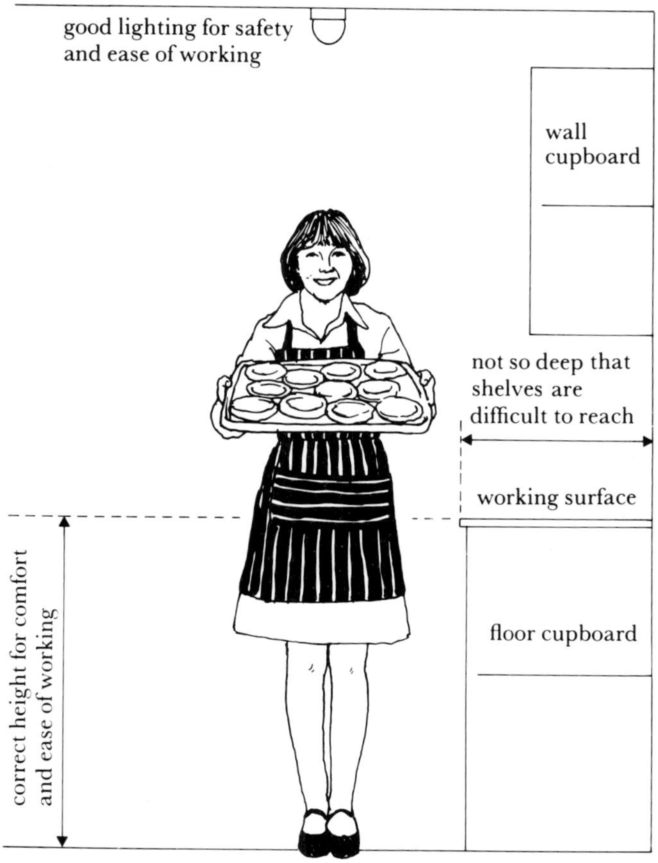


## Cookers

The cooker is the most important piece of equipment in the kitchen. The heat for cooking is usually obtained from one of the following:

a) Gas: natural, coal or Calor
b) Electricity
c) Solid fuel
d) Heating oil.

A cooker consists of an oven for baking, together with a hob or hotplate for boiling, frying, etc., and a grill. It is made of sheet steel with a vitreous enamel finish which is easy to keep clean. About 70% of the heat used in family cooking is supplied by the hotplate, which is usually about 910 mm above floor level. The width and depth of the cooker vary with its size. A wide oven is easier to use than a deep one. The oven, hob and grill may be separate and fitted in different parts of the kitchen.

Gas cookers

The oven is a double walled box of sheet steel with a heat-insulating layer between the walls. It has a well-fitting door;

burners are fitted at the bottom either at the back or the sides. There is a vent to remove the products of combustion. The controls on the oven and rings have numbered or marked dials which operate the thermostats. The hob is usually placed above the oven and contains a set of gas rings and a grill. The grill is sometimes fixed at eye level.

Electric cookers

These resemble gas cookers in design, but the oven is heated from elements usually fitted in the side walls, or sometimes under the floor of the oven. The circulation of air can be improved by a fan fitted in the oven wall, this ensures an even distribution of heat. The hotplate is usually fitted above the oven and has several boiling rings either of the quick heating radiant type or fitted within a smooth, ceramic top. The grill element is a coil of high resistance wire fitted in an insulating plate, the heat being radiated from the red-hot wire down on to the food placed below.

Microwave cookers

The scientific principle of microwave cooking is that electromagnetic energy is absorbed by water in the food and converted to heat.

This is quicker than traditional methods where heat is transferred from an outside source. Water readily absorbs electromagnetic radiation and generates heat, so foods containing plenty of water, evenly distributed, cook well in microwave ovens.

The inside of the oven does not become hot, so the walls are not insulated and the cooker is a compact size.

Metals reflect microwaves so tins cannot be used in microwave ovens. Glass, china, plastic and cardboard all transmit microwaves, i.e. allow them to pass through, so these are suitable materials for cooking dishes.

Uneven distribution of microwaves can cause burnt patches in the centre of food. To avoid this, a metal stirrer in the roof of the oven reflects the microwaves, or a turntable in the base allows the food to be turned continuously.

Browning of food does not occur in microwave cooking as there is no outside source of heat and cooking time is short; the cooking resembles 'dry' steaming in that the food is pale.

Cooked foods can easily be re-heated in a microwave oven, the surface does not dry out as it is heated from within.

Frozen food can be thawed in a microwave oven but as water absorbs the microwaves quicker than ice, the thawing can be uneven and burnt patches can occur in the centre of foods. To avoid this, automatic defrost cycles produce short bursts of microwaves and then pause, to allow the heat generated to be conducted slowly through the food so allowing even thawing.

Microwave ovens are designed to high safety standards, the cooker has two inter-locks which cut off the radiation when the door is opened, and the door fits well so there is no leakage.

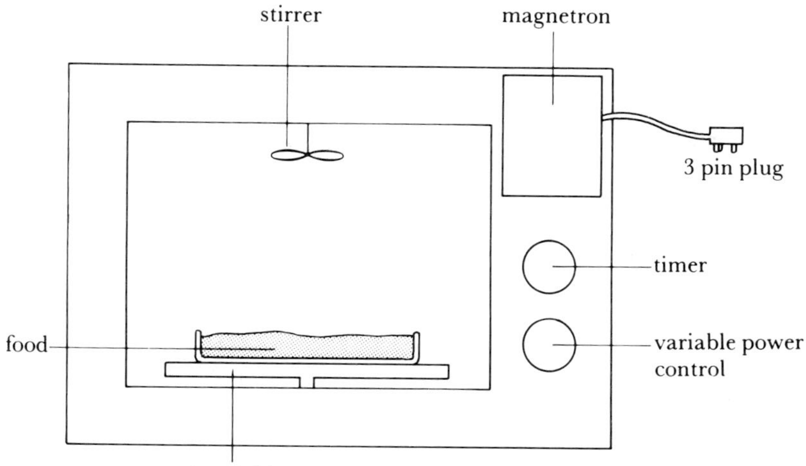

*Microwave cooker*

**Heat-storage cookers**

These may be fired with solid fuel, heating oil or gas. They are solidly constructed, heavily insulated and heated continuously. They can also be used for central heating and hot water. The heavy construction and continuous heating ensures a very even temperature in the ovens which is always instantly available. A thermostat controls the rate of burning and the oven is usually kept at about 205°C–230°C, this temperature cannot be quickly adjusted. A second, cooler oven is often provided, e.g. Aga, Rayburn or Esse cookers.

**How to choose a cooker**

| HOW | WHY |
|---|---|
| *Points to consider:* | |
| 1. *Fuel available*<br>Gas, electricity, oil, coke, anthracite or other smokeless fuel. | Usually all available in towns; gas is sometimes not available in country districts except in portable gas containers. |
| 2. *Use to which it will be put*<br>Whether required for central heating and hot water as well as for cooking. | Only a heat storage cooker will do all three. |
| 3. *Cost*<br>Consider here not only the initial cost but also the running costs of the cooker. | Heat storage cookers are often more expensive to buy but cheaper to run. Gas and electricity are about equal on both counts if used intelligently. |

| HOW | WHY |
|---|---|
| 4. *Size*<br>Great variety available.<br>Choose one large enough for the needs of the family but not too big for the kitchen. | A heat storage cooker really needs a large kitchen. |
| 5. *Efficiency*<br>Gas is quick heating and easily regulated. | Instant heat is available from burning gas, taps regulate flow easily. |
| With electricity the equipment is usually slower to reach working temperature and reacts slowly to any adjustment.<br>A heat storage cooker is always at working temperature but is slow to regulate and more skill is required in using it. | Time must be allowed for the hotplates to heat and to cool. Radiant burners are quicker. |
| 6. *Labour involved in use*<br>Gas and electricity involve very little work, solid fuel needs more. | Work is necessary to refuel, to clear ashes, etc. |
| 7. *Cleanliness in use*<br>Electricity is the cleanest. | No fuel is burnt in an electric stove.<br>The gaseous products of combustion from a gas stove have to be removed.<br>Solid fuel produces dust, ashes and soot, various gases and perhaps smoke if a smokeless fuel is not used. |
| 8. *Ease of cleaning*<br>Most stoves are coated with vitreous enamel. The smooth surfaces of electric and solid fuel cookers are usually more easily cleaned than those of gas burners.<br>Ceramic hobs can only be cleaned when cold. | |
| Some ovens have 'self-clean' linings. | Food residues burn off while the oven is hot. |
| Some ovens have pyrolytic cleaning. | At very high temperatures the food residue is turned to ash. |
| 9. *Appearance*<br>Most modern cookers are neat and of pleasing design. Choose a colour and style to fit the general colour scheme. | With so wide a choice colour and design are purely a personal matter. |

How to use cookers

To achieve good results, to avoid waste of heat and to minimise risk of accidents, the cooker must be used intelligently. The following points must be considered:

| HOW | WHY |
|---|---|
| 1. *Choice of cooking pan* For all solid hotplates a flat bottomed heavy pan is necessary. On electric radiant plates and on gas, a lighter pan may be used. | A good thermal contact is necessary between hotplate and pan for efficient conduction of heat. |
| 2. *Use of hotplate* Allow gas flames to touch bottom of pan, but not to come round the sides. | To minimise loss of heat. |
| On electric plates, have pan large enough to cover the hotplate and switch off before the end of cooking. | To minimise loss of heat. To utilise residual heat in the hotplate. |
| On a heat storage cooker keep hotplate covered when not in use. | To avoid loss of heat. |
| Keep surfaces of hotplates and pans clean. | Grease and dirt are poor heat conductors. Their presence causes a thin film of air between the metal surfaces. |
| Use a pressure cooker when possible. | To economise on fuel. |
| 3. *Use of oven* Always cook as much food as possible at one time, and place in the oven intelligently. | To make best use of oven heat. |
| Use a baking sheet under dishes when possible. | Easier to handle, and this often avoids accidents. |
| Switch off electricity before end of cooking. | Oven stays hot and the available heat can be then utilised. |
| 4. *Safety* Handles of pans, pans with hot fat, etc. on all cookers should be so disposed that accidents cannot occur. | There is risk of burns and scalds if pans are carelessly placed. |
| A child guard can be fitted. | The rail prevents children touching pans or rings. |

| | |
|---|---|
| Check that gas taps are turned off and out of reach of small children. | Gas is poisonous and forms an explosive mixture with air. |
| Check that an electric cooker is 'earthed'. Turn off before cleaning. | To avoid risk of shock. |
| 5. *Cleaning* | |
| Wipe out electric and gas ovens while still warm. | Grease and dirt are easier to remove while warm. |
| Wipe up spilt or splashed food from all cookers immediately. | Easier to remove. |
| For a periodic clean, take out removable parts and clean by washing with hot water and a detergent. (Electric elements must not be made wet.) | |
| Vitreous enamel stoves should be washed, and stubborn marks removed with soap and steel wool with care to avoid scratching. | A coarse abrasive will scratch the surface. |
| Metal parts must be dried thoroughly by heating the stove after cleaning it. | To prevent rust forming. |

Oven temperatures

Every modern cooker is fitted with a thermostat, i.e. a device for keeping the oven at a chosen temperature. This temperature may be selected by turning a dial which shows either the required temperature, or letters or figures which correspond.

*Temperatures in degrees*

| *State of oven* | *Fahrenheit* | *Celsius* | *Dial number* |
|---|---|---|---|
| Cool | 200–250 | 100–130 | ¼–½ |
| Slow | 275–300 | 140–150 | 1–2 |
| Moderate | 325–350 | 170–180 | 3–4 |
| Fairly hot | 375–400 | 190–200 | 5–6 |
| Hot | 425–450 | 220–230 | 7–8 |
| Very hot | 475–500 | 240–260 | 9 |

**Sinks**

Much of the work done in the kitchen is at the sink, which should be supplied with both hot and cold water and a waste pipe for emptying. The sink should be at a convenient height from the ground.

## How to choose a sink

| HOW | WHY |
|---|---|
| 1. *Type* | |
| A sink unit (with fitted draining boards and cupboards) is best. | Economical of space and easy to clean. |
| A double sink is useful. | Rinsing is easier. |
| If the purchase of a complete sink unit is not possible, choose a sink which will take two draining boards, if kitchen space allows. | Easier for washing up. Dirty utensils can be stacked on one side. |
| 2. *Material* | |
| There is a wide choice, e.g. | |
| a) Glazed earthenware. | Cheap, easily cleaned, but easily chipped. |
| b) Metal, e.g. stainless steel. | More expensive but durable and easily cleaned. |
| c) Moulded plastic, e.g. laminated glass fibre. | Durable, easily cleaned, stain resistant, quieter in use and attractive in appearance, but expensive. |
| 3. *Size and shape* | |
| Usually rectangular with curved corners. | For easy cleaning. |
| Deep enough and wide enough. | To avoid splashing surroundings and to take a washing bowl. |
| Of a suitable height. | For comfortable working. |
| 4. *Position and surroundings* | |
| Best position is: | |
| a) On outside wall. | For ease of plumbing. |
| b) Near window. | For good light. |
| c) Near cooker and work-surface. | To save carrying pans. |
| Surroundings must be smooth, e.g. tiles, enamel paint. | For easy cleaning. |
| It is convenient to have cupboards fitted near the sink. | For storing cleaning and laundry materials. |
| 5. *Sink fitments* | |
| a) Taps should be of stainless material. | To save cleaning. |
| Taps should be at least 30 cm from bottom of sink. | For ease of filling buckets, etc. |
| b) Draining boards, of stainless steel, enamel or hardwood should slope towards sink. | To allow water to drain off. |
| c) Overflow outlet, a stopper for the waste pipe, and a grating over the waste outlet should be fitted. | To avoid flooding, blockages, etc. |

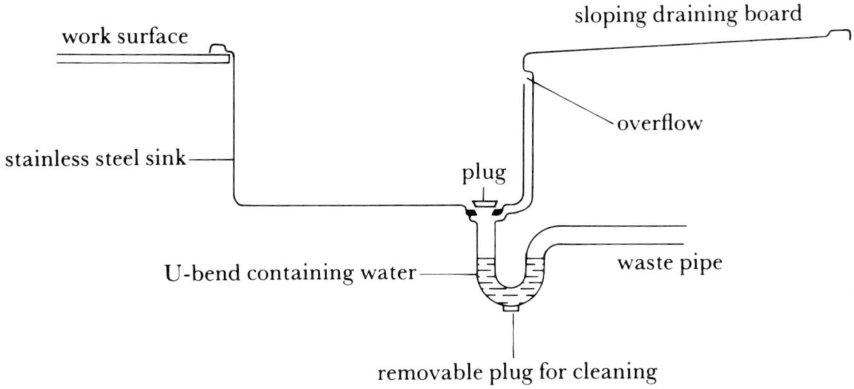


*Section through a sink*

| | HOW | WHY |
|---|---|---|
| How to use and clean a sink | 1. Use a sink-tidy of enamel or polythene. | To collect rubbish and to avoid blocking waste pipe. |
| | 2. Keep very clean, using warm water, detergent and a recommended cleaner. | |
| | 3. Flush with tap water after cleaning. | To leave clean water in U-trap. |
| | 4. Disinfect regularly with bleach. | |
| | 5. If U-trap gets blocked, use a sink plunger, *or*<br>unscrew nut under trap (with a bucket underneath) and clean pipe with a brush. | To remove the trouble by varying the pressure in pipe.<br>To remove blockage. |

## Working surfaces in the kitchen

One or more flat surfaces are necessary in every kitchen for food preparation. The surface may be a table top, the top of a low floor-cupboard, a let-down flap from the wall or a continuation of the sink unit. It should be hard, smooth, stain-resistant, quiet to work on, resistant to cutting edges, pleasant to look at and of reasonable cost. It should be arranged at a convenient height for the user – a very important aid in minimising fatigue.

How to choose and use working surfaces

| HOW | WHY |
|---|---|
| 1. *Position* | |
| They must be near the sink and cooker, must be well lit, of a reasonably large size, and of convenient height, not too wide. | For the convenience of the housewife. Too small a surface cramps the work. To eliminate stretching and stooping. |
| 2. *Material*<br>Choose between: | |
| a) Wood | Cheap, durable, quiet, but needs scrubbing. |
| b) Stainless steel. | Smooth, easily cleaned but noisy in use and expensive. |
| c) Vitreous enamel | Smooth, easily cleaned but noisy in use and chips easily. |
| d) Laminated plastic | Smooth, easily cleaned, stain resistant and pleasant in appearance, but can be scratched, and blistered by heat. |
| 3. *Use*<br>a) Do not chop or cut directly on them but use a hard chopping board. | To maintain working surfaces in good condition. |
| b) Do not place very hot pans or irons on them. Use a stand. | |
| c) Remove all flour, scraps, etc. before washing; wash all surfaces with warm soapy water (scrub the wood the way of the grain); rinse and dry well. Remove stains with scouring powder, or use a mild bleach. | |

**Electrical equipment in the kitchen**

Cookers, refrigerators and freezers are covered in other sections of the book. Other types of electrical equipment used in food preparation are:

1. Mixers, processors, blenders.
2. Kettles, coffee percolators.
3. Toasters.
4. Grills.
5. Fryers: shallow and deep.
6. Slow cookers.
7. Dishwashers.

| Use of electrical equipment | **HOW** | **WHY** |
|---|---|---|
| | 1. *Mixers*:<br>Table top or hand mixers with beaters, whisks or dough hooks. | They reduce time and effort needed for food preparation. Used as instructed they are efficient for rubbed-in, whisked, creamed or dough mixes. |
| | 2. *Processors*:<br>High speed blades combine, slice or chop ingredients. | High speed equipment which, used as instructed, will perform certain processes quickly and efficiently. |
| | 3. *Blenders or liquidisers*:<br>a) reduce semi-solid material to a pulp. | Can be used instead of sieving, e.g. soup making, baby foods. |
| | b) Cut up ingredients. | e.g. bread and herbs for stuffing, oranges and lemons for drinks. |
| | c) Combine ingredients. | e.g. egg yolk, vinegar and oil for mayonnaise. |
| | 4. *Kettles*:<br>To boil water using an immersion element. | Quick and efficient. |
| | 5. *Percolators*:<br>To heat water and percolate ground coffee for a set time. | Quick, efficient infusion of coffee grounds. Ready to serve from percolator. |
| | 6. *Toasters*:<br>To toast bread, pre-set to give correct time. | Quick, efficient, automatic. |
| | 7. *Grills, 'infra-red' or contact*:<br>Compact, portable cookers. | Can be used on any 3 pin socket. Useful for 1 or 2 people, e.g. for toasted sandwiches, steaks, bacon. Can be used to bake food in a tin. |
| | May produce more heat in the infra-red wavelength. | So cooks food more quickly than a traditional grill. |
| | Electric elements heat plates: one forms the base of the cooker, the other forms a hinged lid. | Food cooks on both sides at once, so is cooked quickly. |
| | Heating plates are ridged. | To allow air to circulate and fat to drain away. |

| HOW | WHY |
|---|---|
| 8. *Frypan-oven or multi-cooker*: | |
| Compact, thermostatically controlled pan. Has high domed lid and can be used like a small oven, heated in the base. Versatile. | Can be used on 3 pin socket. Used for frying, boiling, steaming, roasting and some baking. |
| 9. *Deep fat fryer*: | |
| Thermostatically controlled. | Avoids over-heating the fat so making frying safer. |
| Small or large capacity. May have lid which absorbs frying smells. | Choice of sizes for 1–6 people. More pleasant to use than a chip pan. |
| 10. *Slow cookers*: | |
| Large, casserole-type dish surrounded by heating jacket. | |
| All ingredients must be brought to the boil before leaving the cooker on a low setting. | To kill bacteria and to ensure successful cooking at the right temperature. |
| Low electrical consumption. | Economical. |
| Suitable to leave all day while out of the house. | Just enough heat to maintain simmering. |
| 11. *Dishwashers*: | |
| Large machines usually plumbed in to water and drainage system. | Automatic |
| Use a little, very hot water. | Works with high pressure jets of water. |
| Not quick, several rinses and a drying period may be included in the programme. | Very efficient and hygienic. |
| Most china and glass can be safely washed. | Plates and cups are fixed in racks and sprayed with water and detergent. |
| Large pans and dishes may not fit. | Most suitable for up to 12 place settings. |

## Small equipment for the kitchen

When buying small equipment choose:

1. The best quality you can afford. It will last longer.
2. Equipment easy to clean and to keep in repair.
3. Implements which are comfortable to use and of the right size for the work in hand.
4. Those with a good design and with a good finish, pleasant to look at. The quality bought depends upon the amount of cooking to be done.

## Choice and care of kitchen utensils

| EQUIPMENT | CHOICE | CARE |
|---|---|---|
| 1. *Wooden articles* | | |
| Chopping board<br>Rolling pin<br>Wooden spoons<br>Pastry board (unless working surfaces can be used) | Hardwoods, e.g. teak, oak, give better wear. | Scrub the way of the grain, rinse well. Dry in air. Bleach occasionally. |
| 2. *Cloths* | | |
| Oven cloth<br>Floor cloth<br>Tea towels<br>Dish cloth<br>Hand towels | Choose absorbent material which can be easily washed and boiled. | Boil or wash in hot water. Rinse and dry in open air. |
| 3. *Cutlery* | | |
| Vegetable knife<br>Cook's knife and fork<br>Palette knife<br>Potato peeler<br>Kitchen scissors<br>Ladle<br>Fish slice<br>Spoons (3 sizes) | Stainless steel is easy to keep clean but for sharp cutting edges carbon steel is better. For spoons, nickel plate is satisfactory. | Sharpen knives frequently. Wash in hot soapy water, do not soak unless handles are riveted. Remove stains with steel wool. Keep sharp knives in a magnetic or slotted rack. |
| 4. *Earthenware, glass, ovenware or china* | | |
| Mixing bowl<br>Pudding basins<br>Pie dishes<br>Casseroles<br>Jelly moulds<br>Plates | Choose ware with a good protective glaze. Heat resisting glassware is useful. | Soak to remove remains of starchy mixtures. Wash and dry well. |
| 5. *Brushes* | | |
| Pastry brush<br>Vegetable brush<br>Nail brush<br>Small scrubbing brush<br>Pan scourers (may be nylon) | Nylon bristles are easier to keep clean and stiffer than natural bristles. | Wash, rinse in cold water and hang to dry. |
| 6. *Tinware (or aluminium)* | | |
| Roasting tin<br>Baking sheets<br>Cake tins<br>Sandwich tins<br>Bun trays<br>Cooling tray<br>Graters | Choose heavy gauge tinned sheet steel or aluminium. See that tinned steel has no sharp edges. | Wipe while still hot, wash in hot soapy water. Dry well and store in a dry place. |

| | | |
|---|---|---|
| Tin-opener<br>Pastry cutters<br>Whisk<br>Corkscrew,<br>Bottle-opener | Choose a tin-opener which does not call for skill or physical effort on the part of the user. | Keep absolutely clean. |

7. *Pots and pans*

| | | |
|---|---|---|
| Saucepans (at least 3) with lids<br>Kettle<br>Shallow frying pan<br>Deepfryer with lid<br>Steamer (to fit large saucepan) | a) Aluminium, hard-wearing and easy to clean.<br>b) Enamel, which is hard wearing and easy to clean but chips easily.<br>c) Stainless steel, which is excellent but expensive. | Soak immediately after use; burnt pans must be soaked in salt water. Wash in hot soapy water and use steel wool or nylon scourer to remove stains. Rinse and dry well. |

*Note.* Pans must be flat-bottomed for use on solid hotplates, must have heat-resisting handles, well-fitting lids with knobs and be well balanced with wide bases.

8. *Scales, knife sharpener, mincing machines, etc.* are also needed.

9. *Plastic ware*

| | | |
|---|---|---|
| Storage jars<br>Lemon squeezer<br>Flour dredger<br>Liquid measure<br>Colander<br>Strainer<br>Measuring spoons | There is a wide choice in this ware. It is light, pleasant in appearance, easy to clean and not easily broken. | Avoid using them near a source of heat as some may soften and melt. Wash in warm water and dry well. |
| Pudding bowls<br>Washing-up bowl<br>Covered bin for rubbish | Made of polypropylene | Will withstand boiling water. |

10. *Other utensils* (although not really essential) help by saving time. Such things include rotary whisks, food mixers and blenders, egg slicers and pressure cookers. If more elaborate cooking is done, such things as soufflé dishes, forcing bags, dariole moulds and a sugar thermometer are also helpful.

11. *Fire blanket, fire extinguishers, first-aid box.*

## The weighing and measuring of ingredients

For good results in cookery, ingredients should be weighed or, if no scales are available, measured. Many cooks of long experience are capable of estimating with considerable accuracy the amounts of ingredients required, but estimating by guesswork is not a practice to be recommended to the student.

## Weighing

Use reliable scales. There are two main types of scales for domestic use:

1. *Balance scales with weights*: these are the more accurate. The scale pan should move freely before you begin. The correct weight is obtained when the food on the scale pan just balances the weights on the other so that both sides are level.
2. *Spring scales*: the indicator needle should be pointing to zero before you begin. The correct weight is obtained when the indicator needle is pointing to the required weight on the dial.

## Measuring

In America all ingredients are measured by the Standard Cup (8 fluid ounces). The British Standard Cup of 10 fluid ounces has been replaced by a range of cup measures, and there is also a new range of standard spoon sizes. These are:

| | | | | | | |
|---|---|---|---|---|---|---|
| Cup measures: | 50 ml | 75 ml | 100 ml | 150 ml | 300 ml | |
| Spoon measures: | 1.25 ml | 2.5 ml | 5 ml | 10 ml | 15 ml | 20 ml |

Measuring jugs are practical as they provide a range of measures. Usually they are graduated in decilitres but some have smaller graduations. Many are marked to give approximate measure of dry ingredients such as sugar and flour, though it must be remembered that these are not always very accurate.

*Measuring liquids*: Spoon or cup measures should be filled until they are almost overflowing. Measuring jugs should be placed on a flat surface and the reading taken at eye level to ensure as much accuracy as possible.

*Measuring dry ingredients*: The terms 'level', 'rounded' and 'heaped' spoonfuls are often used. The diagram shows what is meant by these. Many people use ordinary household spoons for measuring but since these are not in standard sizes, the results may be unsatisfactory. Obviously, level spoonfuls are more accurate measures than rounded or heaped spoonfuls. If using a measuring jug, this should be shaken gently so that the dry ingredient will level off, before the reading is taken.

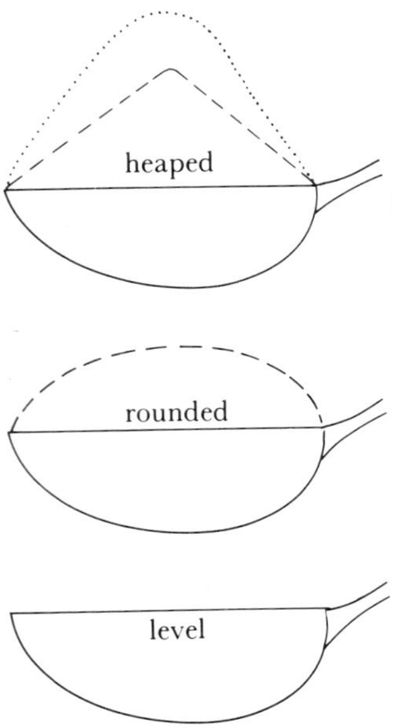


*Some handy measures*

With dry ingredients, the number of spoonfuls which make up a given weight will vary according to the density of the ingredient being measured. The following is a rough guide:

| | | |
|---|---|---|
| 1 tablespoon (15 ml) water, milk or other liquid | = | 20 g |
| 1 tablespoon jam, honey, syrup or treacle | = | 25 g |
| 1 rounded tablespoon flour, cornflour, cocoa or custard powder | = | 20 g |
| 1 rounded tablespoon sugar | = | 25 g |
| 1 rounded tablespoon rice, dried fruit | = | 30 g |

The 50 ml measuring cup holds 50 g sugar.
The 75 ml measuring cup holds 50 g flour.
Packaged fats weighing 250 g can be divided into 25 g portions by marking off into ten divisions.

# Glossary of special terms

*Refer to the index if the term you want is not in this glossary.*

## Chemical terms

**Atoms** The smallest particles of an element which can take part in a chemical reaction.

**Molecules** The smallest particles of a substance that are capable of independent existence.

**Elements** Pure substances in which all atoms are similar. They cannot be broken down (decomposed) by chemical means into simpler substances. Examples are: sodium, chlorine, carbon, hydrogen, oxygen.

**Mineral elements** These occur in the soil and are taken up by plants during growth; they differ from nitrogen and the organic elements carbon, hydrogen and oxygen. They are frequently metals in their uncombined state although in foods they exist as mineral compounds or salts. These substances make up the ash which remains when animal or plant tissues are burnt.

**Compounds** Substances composed of two or more elements combined together in fixed proportions. Examples are: carbon dioxide, sodium chloride.

**Ions** Atoms or parts of molecules which carry an electric charge, e.g. chloride ions, sodium ions.

**Acids** Substances which dissolve in water with the formation of hydrogen ions. Acids turn blue litmus red, e.g. tartaric acid, citric acid, lactic acid.

**Alkalis** Substances which dissolve in water with the formation of hydroxyl ions, they turn red litmus to blue, e.g. sodium hydroxide, sodium hydrogen carbonate.

**pH** This is a convenient method of expressing the acidity or alkalinity of solutions: the range is from acid pH 0 to alkaline pH 14, with neutral as pH 7.

**Salts** Compounds formed when acids and alkalis react, or when a metal replaces the hydrogen in an acid. Some salts are acid in solution, e.g. potassium hydrogen tartrate (cream of tartar), and acid calcium phosphate. Some salts are alkaline in solution, e.g. sodium hydrogen carbonate (bicarbonate of soda). Some salts are insoluble in water, e.g. iron phytate.

## Biological terms

**Digestion** The chemical breakdown of large nutrient molecules into simple, soluble substances that can be absorbed by the body.

**Absorption** The transfer of the digested nutrients from the intestines into the body, either into the bloodstream or the lymphatic system.

**Metabolism** The sum total of all the chemical and physical changes taking place in living matter. In nutrition these changes are concerned with the use of nutrients by the body.

**Basal metabolism** (See Energy page 16.)

**Basal metabolic rate** The amount of energy used in a given time just to keep the body alive while at rest, i.e. for circulation, breathing, body temperature and other chemical reactions in the body.

**Catalyst** A substance which speeds up a chemical reaction but at the end remains unchanged itself.

**Enzyme** A catalyst produced by a living cell which speeds up a chemical reaction that would otherwise take place slowly. An enzyme is specific, it only catalyses one reaction, e.g. maltase will only act on maltose to split it into two molecules of glucose.

## Terms used in food preparation

**Basting** Pouring liquid from a spoon over food during cooking, usually hot fat during roasting.

**Blanching** The food to be blanched, or 'whitened', is boiled in water 1–2 minutes and then strained. It is used to remove the brown skins from almonds. Also it is used to inactivate enzymes in vegetables prior to freezing (see page 133).

**Blending** Mixing smoothly, usually a starchy powder with an equal volume of cold liquid, prior to mixing it with boiling liquid, e.g. custard powder and milk. Also it is used to mean mixing smoothly in an electric blender or liquidiser, sometimes used to make soups or fruit purées.

**Breadcrumbs** Fresh white breadcrumbs are used in toppings (*au gratin*), for stuffings, in bread sauce and to lighten suet pudding mixtures. They can easily be made by dropping pieces of bread on to the moving knives in an electric blender or liquidiser. If this is not available stale bread can be grated.

**Coating** Covering with a thin layer of a thickened liquid, such as batter or sauce, or with egg and dry breadcrumbs. A coating sauce should coat the back of a spoon and just find its own level in the pan. Use it while it is hot.

**Croutons** Small dice of fried or toasted bread, eaten as an accompaniment to soup. Larger, neatly cut pieces can be used to garnish food cooked with a sauce.

| | |
|---|---|
| **Glaze** | A thin, shiny coating which may be of egg and milk on baked goods, e.g. bread rolls; or sugar syrup on buns; or fruit juice thickened with arrowroot on fruit gateaux. |
| **Au gratin** | Derived from the French 'gratter' – to scratch, and means a rough, crumbly surface browned under a grill; it does not necessarily contain cheese although it may do so. |
| **Process** | To take natural, fresh foods and change their nature in some way to make a different food product, e.g. wheat grains are processed into wheat flake breakfast cereals which are ready-to-eat. Tough, fatty cuts of meat can be processed into sausages, hamburgers or other convenient forms. |
| **Purée** | A smooth pulp usually of vegetables or fruit made by sieving or in an electric liquidiser. Also the name of a group of soups made with sieved ingredients. |
| **Raspings** | Dried, sieved breadcrumbs used for egg and breadcrumb coating. To make raspings, dry stale scraps of bread in a slow oven, crush them in a bag with a rolling pin and sift them. Store them in an airtight tin. |
| **Refine** | To remove 'rough' or unwanted parts to make a purer form. This makes unnaturally concentrated types of food, e.g. fats such as butter, lard and oils; sugar; white flour. |
| **Zest** | The oil which gives the flavour to orange and lemon peel. To use the zest, the peel is taken off so thinly that it is yellow on both sides with no pith, or it is grated finely so that only the shiny yellow part of the rind is scraped off. |

# Index